Post-Traumatic Jesus

Post-Traumatic Jesus

A Healing Gospel
for the Wounded

DAVID W. PETERS

WESTMINSTER
JOHN KNOX PRESS
LOUISVILLE · KENTUCKY

First edition
Published by Westminster John Knox Press
Louisville, Kentucky

23 24 25 26 27 28 29 30 31 32—10 9 8 7 6 5 4 3 2 1

Unless otherwise indicated, Scripture quotations are from the New Revised Standard Version of the Bible, copyright © 1989 by the Division of Christian Education of the National Council of the Churches of Christ in the U.S.A., and are used by permission. Scripture quotations marked ESV are from the *The Holy Bible, English Standard Version,* © 2001 by Crossway Bibles, a publishing ministry of Good News Publishers. Used by permission. All rights reserved. Scripture quotations marked RSV are from the Revised Standard Version of the Bible, copyright © 1946, 1952, 1971, and 1973 by the Division of Christian Education of the National Council of the Churches of Christ in the U.S.A., and are used by permission.

Book design by Drew Stevens
Cover design by Stephen Brayda

Library of Congress Cataloging-in-Publication Data

Names: Peters, David W., author.
Title: Post-traumatic Jesus : a healing gospel for the wounded / David W. Peters.
Description: First edition. | Louisville, Kentucky : Westminster John Knox Press, [2023] | Summary: "For thousands of years, Jesus' wounds, both visible and invisible, have been a way to know him and find healing in a traumatized world. This book examines the Gospels through the lens of trauma, in hopes that the reader will meet the post-traumatic Jesus and feel his love"-- Provided by publisher.
Identifiers: LCCN 2022051838 (print) | LCCN 2022051839 (ebook) | ISBN 9780664267322 (paperback) | ISBN 9781646983032 (ebook)
Subjects: LCSH: Suffering--Religious aspects--Christianity.
Classification: LCC BT732.7 .P434 2023 (print) | LCC BT732.7 (ebook) | DDC 231/.8--dc23/eng/20230117
LC record available at https://lccn.loc.gov/2022051838
LC ebook record available at https://lccn.loc.gov/2022051839

Most Westminster John Knox Press books are available at special quantity discounts when purchased in bulk by corporations, organizations, and special-interest groups. For more information, please e-mail SpecialSales@wjkbooks.com.

To the people of St. Joan of Arc Episcopal Church.
It is good to be in the side-wound of Jesus with you.

Contents

Content warning: *Several chapters in this book discuss violence, rape, abuse, and self-harm.*

Acknowledgments

When the COVID-19 pandemic began, I thought I would write several creative books from the isolation of my home. I also thought I would finally achieve my best marathon time with "nothing else to do." I thought I'd get in the best shape of my life! I did a few "around the house marathons" and then quit running for a year. I also found myself profoundly uncreative. It was all I could do to tune in to the latest awful news story, then tune out.

It was during this time that I started working on this book, which had been percolating in my mind ever since I published *Post-Traumatic God*. With the insight and encouragement of Valerie Weaver-Zercher, this book came into being. I'm so thankful to Westminster John Knox Press for publishing it, and for the sharp and insightful editorial skills of Jessica Miller Kelley, who made this book so much better for the reader. Kathleen Niendorff, my agent, kept me writing through some very difficult times, and she always challenges me to keep swimming.

Much of this book emerged from a course I taught at Seminary of the Southwest in Austin, Texas, a few years ago, "Ministry to People with PTSD." It's likely I learned more from my students than they learned from me, and I'm thankful they are out in the field today. Thanks be to God for seminaries like SSW that teach their students about trauma.

I'm thankful for my family and all the brilliant writers whose encouragement and friendship have inspired me to keep going, notably Chris Tomlinson, Logan Isaac, Mary Lowery,

Bryan Mealer, and Keri Blakinger. I'm thankful to the people of St. Joan of Arc Episcopal Church, a new church plant I've had the honor to shepherd. Most of what I have learned about the post-traumatic Jesus I have learned from them.

Introduction

The post-traumatic Jesus is the only Jesus Christianity has ever known. In Greek, *trauma* means "wound," a tearing of the flesh, or, metaphorically, an injury to the soul. From Thomas who wants to touch Jesus' wounds to the Moravians who described their church services as "being in the wound," the wounded, traumatized Jesus brings healing and hope to traumatized people. While other, more sanitized versions of Jesus have been presented over time, often by people of great privilege, it is the post-traumatic Jesus who has endured. Indeed, in recent years we have witnessed a variety of perspectives on Jesus, including Black, liberationist, mujerista, womanist, and feminist perspectives to counter the white- and male-centric versions of Jesus that have been presented over time, often by men of great privilege. As a white male myself, I realize I have so much to learn from these perspectives, many of which process the trauma of Jesus' life through their own traumatic experiences.

Ever since I came back from the Iraq War, I've read Scripture through a post-traumatic lens. This reading has not only helped me process my own traumatic experiences but also offers a window into how the original writers of the Gospels understood the story of Jesus and how the original readers read these texts. The brutal Roman military occupation of Jesus' homeland, the First Jewish-Roman War of AD 66, and the unrelenting violence of a world lit only by fire were ever present in the minds of Jesus' hearers and the early Christians who followed him, many to their own traumatic deaths. This book examines the stories in the Gospels through the lens of trauma, paying careful attention to how the authors used these stories to cultivate hope and healing for traumatized people, preserving the story of the post-traumatic Jesus who extends his wounded hands to us.

Until now, reading Scripture through the lens of trauma has been an academic discipline. In 2016, the Society of Biblical Literature published *Bible through the Lens of Trauma,* a collection of essays exploring this way of reading Scripture.[1]

In 2012, a conference, "Trauma and Traumatization: Biblical Studies and Beyond," was held at Aarhus University, Denmark, contributing significantly to the field. I hope this book bridges the gap between this scholarship and the readers who need to know they are not alone in their post-traumatic world. Furthermore, I hope this book will help you see your traumatic experiences as having spiritual significance, a point often overlooked in trauma therapy.

The study of trauma is constantly evolving, as is the public discussion of it and how it affects people. In my lifetime, the events of 9/11 and the Afghanistan and Iraq wars that followed made PTSD a household term. Since 2016, the COVID-19 pandemic and the civil unrest after the police killings of Black people have revealed to the general public how trauma can be experienced across communities. The collective experience of racism after 400 years of slavery, Jim Crow, mass incarceration (sometimes called the New Jim Crow), and more can be considered a form of complex PTSD (C-PTSD)—the type that affects hostages and those who have endured long-term domestic abuse.

We have all been traumatized by this pandemic, if not by the disease and death itself then by the callous disregard for human life from those who have not taken it seriously. The threat of an invisible killer in supermarkets, schools, churches, and our relatives' living rooms leaves us hypervigilant at the sound of a sneeze or cough. Stories of moral injury in health-care workers and the subsequent suicides are starting to emerge. Moral injury is a component of trauma for caregivers. The feeling that "I should have done more" or "If only I had done X instead of Y, this person would be alive," can be overwhelming. One only needs to listen in on a nurse telling a family member not to come to the hospital as their loved one dies to feel the weight of moral injury. Jesus was a healer, and his healings addressed not only the physical symptoms but the spiritual and emotional symptoms too. His lonely but public death also stands in solidarity with the victims of COVID-19 who say good-bye on FaceTime as a nurse holds the iPad with a trembling hand.

Add to the pandemic the assault on the U.S. Capitol seen live on TV, the vacuum of withdrawal of our military from Afghanistan, and the relentless toll of mass shootings by lone gunmen trying to make their ideological points by murdering schoolchildren and supermarket shoppers. Stories of domestic abuse, sexual assault and harassment, and child abuse where the perpetrators often go unpunished all take their collective toll on our minds and hearts, and we wonder if it will ever end. The impact on specific victims is worse than our secondary trauma, but it is often equally debilitating. We wonder, Are things getting worse? Unaware that one of the signature wounds of trauma is a foreshortened future where we cannot see anything good ever happening to us again, it is the death of hope we grieve, although we cannot always name it.

Religion has never been perceived as less relevant to people's day-to-day lives than it is today. Mainline churches lament how far attendance has fallen from the crowded Sunday schools of yesteryear and wonder what gimmick they can pull to lure in young families. Meanwhile, Americans seem to be OK as they sip coffee and read the *New York Times* or schlep the kids to a soccer game on a Sunday morning. For many, the only time they have an intense thought about religion is when they recoil

at seeing far-right evangelicals praising Trump or his surro-
gates, or saying God sent COVID-19 because of abortion and
the gays. There are many reasons for the decline in organized
religion, but one is clearly the failure of many churches to gen-
uinely connect the gospel to people's most wounded parts.

For too long, preaching and writing about the crucifixion have been uncomfortable in progressive Christian circles,
mainly for fear that it highlights the penal substitutionary atone-
ment theory that is likened to child abuse of God the Father
upon the Son. I hope this book presents the post-traumatic
Jesus in such a way that Christians can reclaim this territory
from the fundamentalists, who have shamed too many into
praying the sinner's prayer. The goal of this book is to connect
the secular and religious Jesus with contemporary traumatic
experiences so that readers can connect their own stories to
Jesus' story. This is no easy task, as the Jesus of history has
been gilded and gelded with both religious and secular themes
that move traumatized people further from the Jesus who was
nailed to a cross by Roman soldiers and left to die for six hours
on a Friday afternoon. We have to face the trauma of our lives
head on, and the people of Jesus' time knew trauma.

Rome was brutal in a way it is hard to imagine today. Every
soldier of Rome was a killer, a disciplined fighting machine.
These soldiers stayed in formation and threw their javelins.
The javelins had thin steel necks so if they missed, they would
bend out of shape upon impact with the ground, rendering
them unusable by the enemy. If they hit an enemy shield,
they would make the shield unwieldy, and soon thrown to
the ground. Then Rome closed in on the enemy. The Span-
ish sword was short, thick, and sharp. Each legionnaire trained
with it every day, ready to wound its victims with gashes and
meat cleaver-like chops. The damage it inflicted on human
bodies recalls the machete-hacked bodies in mass graves in the
Rwandan Genocide.

The survivors of Rome's wars were sold into slavery. During major campaigns, the huge numbers of enslaved people
would flood the market, driving down prices. Some went to

the mines, some to the fields, and some to the beds of their masters. To be a slave was to lose all bodily autonomy. Slaves had no rights in ancient Rome and could be tortured, beaten, raped, and crucified. There was no escape or rebellion. Spartacus tried this and failed spectacularly and heroically. He died in the final battle, and soon 6,000 of his followers were crucified along the Appian Way, their vulture-picked bodies bearing witness that Rome's war machine always wins.

Jesus was born in a Roman province, just another little life consumed by Rome's gluttonous appetite, and ultimately crucified like so many rebels for daring to defy the ultimate power of the Roman war machine embodied by the emperor.

Many years ago, my four-year-old son came home from preschool upset. When I asked him about it, he said, "My friends laughed at me, they pushed me, then they put me on the cross." He spread his arms wide. I didn't know what to say. What could I say? He understood the symbol in a way that it would take me many years to understand. Even after serving in the army during the Iraq War in Baghdad, coming home to a shattered marriage, and acting out my untreated PTSD on everyone around me, I couldn't do what my son did—to see my trauma somehow being connected to Jesus' traumatic life. But as my certainty in God disappeared in the fog of trauma, my connection to the cross became stronger. Now I read the Gospels through my own post-traumatic lens, and so many of the stories now make more sense to me.

For this reason, we begin at the end, with the lens through which the rest of Jesus' story is viewed—and our stories too. Like the writers of the four Gospels, I also read my own life's story through the lens of my trauma. In many ways, our trauma is the beginning of our story, but it is not the end of our story. The post-traumatic Jesus I see through the lens of my own trauma has drawn me to himself. Perhaps he will draw you too.

1
Skull Hill

We can see Skull Hill now, a macabre place if there ever was one. It was called *Golgotha*, Aramaic for "skull." In Greek it is *Kraníon*—"cranium," in our modern anatomy class. With the Romans we call it *Calvariæ*, for it is like the dome of bone on a human head.

The Jolly Roger pirate flag, the Punisher sticker on a pickup truck window, Dan Aykroyd's personal vodka brand—all skulls. The *Totenkopf* (literally, "dead's head") was the last thing that Jews, crowded into the gas chamber, saw on the collar of the SS guard as he peered through the dirty glass. You will find skulls on countless military unit insignias the world over, as well as on bottles of poisonous liquids and countless other places. Shakespeare's Hamlet holds up a skull and says, "Alas, poor Yorick! I knew him," and the despair and sadness of death is visible.[1] Skulls remind us of our impending death. As we look into the hollow eye sockets, they look into us.

And so Skull Hill is a fitting place for a Roman crucifixion. A plaque written in Aramaic, Greek, and Latin is nailed to the top of the middle cross. It proclaims, "Jesus of Nazareth, King of the Jews." And beneath that multilingual placard hangs a crucified man.

His body is nailed to the wooden beams of the Roman torture device. His eyelids are swollen nearly shut from being beaten about the head. There is a crust of dried blood on his skin, and new blood oozes with each fainting heartbeat. He is alive, thus in *excruciating* pain, crucifixion being at the root of this word for unbearable pain.

Beneath his cross the soldiers who did the actual work of crucifixion are rolling bone dice for his cloak. They are drinking cheap wine, soldier wine, to take the edge off. They have gotten drunk in many lands and far-flung territories of their empire. With every sip, every buzz, every loud war story, they numb all feeling and sympathy for what they do. They take another drink, in hopes this drunk will touch the sadness down below the cruelty. They jokingly offer some to the man on the cross. How could they not have heard that his first miracle was turning water to fine wine at a wedding?

Others insult the crucified man, taunting him with his powerlessness over what is happening to him. Some spit, others stare. Some women are there, his mother and some others. From the nails of the cross, the crucified man speaks through his pain, "Woman, here is your son," and to the disciple John, "Here is your mother" (John 19:26–27). He is asking his friend to watch over her, she who bore him into the world and gave him his first bath. She says nothing. What could she say in the trauma of the moment? Her silence is our silence in the face of horror. He is powerless. She is powerless. It is hard to tell who is in the most pain.

His dehydrated mouth croaks words, and the crowd cannot understand him. Eventually they hear, "I thirst," and someone runs and gets a sponge. The sponge, a carcass of a sea creature who is rooted to one place for life, only to be plucked up by divers and used to clean, is that day dipped in the soldier wine and mixed with a bitter substance that may numb his pain a bit. The act of mercy is a double-edged sword, as the crucified man never knows if it will relieve pain or prolong pain.

There is a loud cry, and he dies. Six hours is short for the torture of the cross. It seems too short, too good to be true for the
bureaucrats who want all the bodies down from the cross before
the approaching festival. They cannot take down live bodies, for
then the victims would not have died by crucifixion. Their sentence of death by torture must be carried out in all its details.
The morality of torture is rigid, exacting, precise, and completely
devoid of human love. A spear is rammed into his side by a soldier to confirm his death. The fluids that gush forth from his
body cavity confirm his clinical death in their death-filled minds.

The trauma of Jesus, often called his passion—these grue-
some six traumatic hours on a Friday afternoon on Skull
Hill—are reenacted, rehearsed, recited, and remembered by
over a billion people during Holy Week every year. A mother
writes a note to her son's principal excusing him from class so
he can walk the stations of the cross with his youth group. A
grandfather kneels in an empty church thumbing a rosary with
a crucifix at its center. A construction worker cuts 4x4s in his
garage with a circular saw to shape into a cross and put on the
lawn of his Baptist church.

Add to these billion all those who have meditated on this
story in the two millennia before us—refugees, soldiers, kings,
peasants. This symbol of a crucified man is placed above the
cradles of babies and on coffins, hot cross buns, and Affliction
T-shirts, as well as tattooed on human skin. It is this symbol
that the burning Joan of Arc begged to be placed before her
as she died in the fire. It is this symbol, the first depiction of
Jesus we have, that some joker carved on the wall of a Roman
house around AD 200. The picture is of a crucified jackass
with a man named Alexamenos, a Christian, looking up at it.
The words "Alexamenos worships [his] god" bear witness to
the young man's absurd faith. The cross is the symbol that an
ICU nurse prays before in the hospital chapel while she tells me
she has always planned her own suicide so she will not have to
die with a tube jammed down her throat.

The cross speaks to our human condition better than most
other symbols. A helpless victim, an unjust trial, a gleeful

cruelty, a silent god—these are not only what happened at the crucifixion; they are the hallmarks of traumatic experiences that most humans experience in our short lives.

While the teachings of Jesus about not worrying and about being kind, and the actions of Jesus such as turning water into wine are wholesome and exemplary, these stories of his life and teachings recorded in the four Gospels were written through the post-traumatic lens of his crucifixion. The Gospel writers knew how the story ends. One of Christianity's earliest theologians, St. Paul, preached very little about Jesus' parables and life events. He had one central message, "We proclaim Christ crucified" (1 Cor. 1:23). While this message was offensive and foolish to many who heard it, it drew a dedicated band of followers from enslaved people and the lowest classes of society, all of whom would have had significant trauma from living on the bottom rungs of the Roman social ladder.

As Mary Beard writes in her monumental work *SPQR,* the Roman world was terrifyingly vicious and is alien to us: "That means not just the slavery, the filth (there was hardly any such thing as refuse collection in ancient Rome), the human slaughter in the arena, and the death from illnesses whose cures we now take for granted; but also the newborn babies thrown away on rubbish heaps, the child brides and the flamboyant eunuch priests."[2] We cannot underestimate how traumatizing this reality was for people living in the world of Jesus. The loss of their political autonomy and judicial recourse, the violent moods of occupying soldiers, and the inability to get ahead because of the tax burden are just a few ways the Romans traumatized the people in Jesus' world. This traumatized world was where the stories of Jesus first circulated, offering a compelling alternative to Rome's violent, traumatizing presence.

2

Announcing the Prince of Peace in a World of War

"They make a desolation and call it peace," Tacitus records barbarian king Calgacus saying before a battle with the Romans in what is now Scotland.[1] Calgacus's speech catalogs the Roman method of conquest, "These plunderers of the world, after exhausting the land by their devastations, are rifling the ocean: stimulated by avarice, if their enemy be rich; by ambition, if poor; unsatiated by the East and by the West: the only people who behold wealth and indigence with equal avidity. To ravage, to slaughter, to usurp under false titles, they call empire; and where they make a desert, they call it peace."[2]

Calgacus loses the battle with the Romans, but his words echo down through history, summarizing the raw feelings of the people who were consumed by Rome's voracious appetite for new land and more tribute money to increase the personal wealth of Rome's old families.

Around sixty years before Jesus' birth, as Julius Caesar is marching his troops through the foggy forests of Britain, the fate of Roman Judea is decided. After a series of battles between the Seleucid king Mithridates VI and the Roman commander Pompey, Rome wins. Shortly after this Roman victory, a dispute between rival Jewish priest-kings, Aristobulus and Hyrcanus, brings Pompey and his legions to Jerusalem. It is here, in 63 BC, that Pompey becomes one of the few men in history to step foot in the Holy of Holies in the Jewish Temple and thereby desecrate it. It would not be the last time Rome defiled the sacred spaces of the Jewish people.

The Temple rises above the bustling city, a giant prayer built of white stone. In it are the hopes, dreams, and fears of Judea and her children who, by the time of Jesus, are found on the three continents of the known world. Its continual smoke of sacrifice ascends, the sizzling steaks and briskets from a thousand oxen causing mouths to water all over the city. Stomach growls ascend to heaven like the ecstatic prayers of mystics.

The Romans have no interest in Jewish religion and no interest in Jews. They have no interest in anything but the cash flowing to their mighty capital. The Romans are not as interested in conquering the world as they are in taxing the world. Many nations simply surrender without a fight; they know the brutality with which the Romans wage war.

It seemed like no one could stop Rome's war machine, not even God.

Many had called on their gods and goddesses when Rome was at the gates, and not one of them could do a thing. When Yahweh destroyed Pharaoh's army in the Red Sea, God's people sang, "Yahweh is a mighty warrior." But where was Yahweh when Roman army boots with their sharp-nailed treads stamped into the Holy of Holies? Where was God when everything collapsed? Where was God on my one worst day?

This question hangs like a gloomy cloud over human history with its battlefields, smoking ruins, refugees delivering babies on the side of the road and trying to walk on. The question comes to us in the evil hours when we stare our losses in the face. Where was God that day, we ask. And all we hear is silence.

Silence, God's first language, mocks us as we struggle to make sense of the traumatic events that turn our world upside down. "My God, my God, why have you forsaken me?" is the first line of Psalm 22, a psalm many in Jesus' day may have prayed as they woke up to the harsh reality of Roman occupation.

The answer to this question that echoes down through time and human misery comes to a town in Galilee called Nazareth. Galilee is a region of northern Palestine distinguished by its hills and the fierce, warlike people who live there. Jewish historian Josephus says the Galileans are fierce fighters. Two of Jesus' disciples are called "Sons of Thunder," and Peter, a Galilean, is the only person to attack with a sword in the New Testament.

Nazareth in Galilee is an obscure place on the world stage. It is far from Rome and far from Jerusalem. It is far from everything. As Nathaniel says in John's Gospel, "Can anything good come out of Nazareth?" (1:46). In the town of Nazareth lived a woman named Mary, who was engaged to a man named Joseph. This is how Luke, our only narrator of these events, introduces them to us. How did they meet? What were their childhoods like? What kind of relationship did they have? We do not know. All we know is their names and where they fit into the story of Jesus' birth, a story that is spare on personal details, the kind of details about human relationships we long for.

It is impossible to know for certain what the people in the world of Jesus felt, but we can be sure they were feeling characters, like us, experiencing sorrow, joy, grief, and delight. While we live in a world where we buy our chicken skinless, boneless, and wrapped in cellophane, theirs was far more bloody and earthy. Their world was also quieter—so much quieter, in the absence of planes, trains, and automobiles, not to mention air conditioners, heaters, and podcasts. The barking of dogs, the squeals of children, and the rooster's crow were their loud noises of life. How much more did they hear than we do in our cacophony? Despite these differences, I believe that we are more similar to these biblical people than we are different. I believe that the human beings in the first century AD experienced traumatic events similarly to the way we do. Jonathan Shay's books *Achilles in Vietnam* and *Odysseus in America* have shown that combat trauma in Homer's day, 1,000 years before

Jesus was born, was eerily similar to combat trauma in our day. Their songs of grief and loss resonate today, as do the psalms and other emotionally laden laments of the ancient world. And so our quest in this book is to feel something with them, so we can understand Jesus better.

We are introduced to Mary with just one key detail—the most intimate detail of her life: that she is a virgin. How she became pregnant prior to her marriage to Joseph is clearly a matter of some debate. There is a tale told by an early enemy of Christianity, Celus, that Mary had a sexual relationship with a Roman soldier named Panther (Latin, *Pantera*), who fathered Jesus. While Panther was a common name for Roman soldiers at that time, this is clearly a second-century urban legend. However, that Greeks and Romans could imagine such a thing helps us understand the world Jesus lived in. Could Mary say no to a Roman soldier who wanted to have sex with her? Not safely. Rape has always been an unofficial strategy in war. The Roman god of war, Mars, is a rapist. His rape of Rhea Silvia produces the twins, Romulus and Remus, the founders of Rome.

It is into this world that the angel Gabriel announces to Mary she will conceive in her womb and bear a son named Jesus. Mary, who is nearly helpless before the rapacious men of Rome, is asked by God to consent.

"Here am I, the slave girl of the Lord, let it be with me according to your word." I translate *doula* as "slave girl," because that is what it meant in the context of the day. Too many translators have softened the impact of this word in the New Testament by translating it "servant." Even "handmaid" sounds gross in light of the Margaret Atwood book and TV adaptation. The word grates against our senses, disturbs, provokes. But this is what she says to the angel, and hence to God. She says yes.

In situations of trauma, especially sexual trauma, the inability to refuse or give consent is the deepest part of the wound. Judith Hermon, in her book *Trauma and Recovery*, tells how an emergency room doctor examines and cares for victims. Every care must be taken in hopes the victim is not "re-raped." The doctor says, "So when I do an examination I spend a lot of time preparing the victim; every step along the way I try to give back control to the victim. I might say, 'We would like to do this and how we do it is your decision,' and provide a large amount of information, much of which I'm sure is never processed; but it still comes across as concern on our part. I try to make the victim an active participant to the fullest extent possible."[3]

The world was brutal before Rome, but Rome industrialized brutality, incentivizing the rapacious and greedy to take more and more. For all those in Jesus' day who were helpless in the face of their violations, the story of the Annunciation, the announcement, is a story where the God of power and might, the Lord of Hosts (armies), waits patiently for the answer of a young woman in an obscure town called Nazareth. Like the ER doctor, God offers a relationship of participation to Mary, and to us as well.

This is where the story of Jesus starts, in a request for consent and a kind of mutuality between God and humanity that is entirely new in the mythologies of the world. This encounter between a god and a human woman that focuses on human reproduction is not new in the stories of the world. Apollo preys on virgins in their prayers, Cassandra being the most famous. She refuses to sleep with him, and so he blesses her with the gift of prophecy, but with the catch that no one will believe her. The rest of her life she is tortured by visions of her city and family burning, but she is seen as a mad woman, hysterical and thus ignored, as all women are when they warn the world of its deserved doom.

In Genesis, the primal account of our origin, we see in chapter 6 that certain angels, "the sons of god," saw that the daughters of humans were beautiful, and so they took them as wives. The word for "take" is the Hebrew word *lacach* and is better translated "seize." In the prophet Samuel's speech about the dangers of getting a king, he warns the people that the king will *lacach* their cattle and donkeys, young men and women, for himself. And so these women were seized and possessed by these wicked angels. The children born to them were giants, Nephilim, and full of violence. These giants traumatized the people of earth until Noah's flood wiped them out, their disembodied souls roaming for a place to inhabit and terrorize.

What we see in the story of the Annunciation is the reversal of how gods relate to humans. We see a reversal of abuse and rape, the reversal of how women and the vulnerable have been seized, used, and disposed of. We see a God who is trying to not, as the ER doctor said, "re-rape" us.

God is initiating this new relationship with Mary and all humanity in the midst of the desolation of the Romans that they call peace. The silence of God is broken. Here is the first word that answers the question "Where were you on my worst day?"

3

Post-Traumatic Christmas

The original Christmas story starts out unromantically with a tax. Emperor Augustus calls for it, and bureaucrats such as Governor Quirinius of Syria, the regional governor of Jesus' family, carry it out. The order of a Roman emperor was to be obeyed by even the most obscure people of his empire, like Jesus' parents, Mary and Joseph.

The Romans did not have kings; they killed them long ago to form a republic that lasted until the general Julius Caesar declared himself to be sole dictator of the empire. From that day on, just a few decades before the birth of Jesus, Rome had emperors—from *imperator*, a word meaning "conqueror." Emperors had always to conquer more territory, thus increasing the tax revenue for the elite residents of Rome. The taxes also fed and equipped Rome's massive army and navy, thus creating a self-perpetuating cycle of consumption.

In Luke's Gospel, we meet Caesar Augustus, the emperor at the time of Jesus' birth. Of course, we do not meet the man, only his name. Caesar was a title adopted by Julius Caesar's successor, Octavian. By taking this title, Octavian took the power and prestige of Julius, thus showing his subjects that he could do to them what Julius did to them if they rebelled and defied his authority. The power of this name, this title, echoes down through history, as it was adapted by different leaders who wanted to conquer like Rome. The kaisers of Prussia, the czars of Russia, even the Ottoman sultans of Turkey adopted the title when they finally overtook the Roman city of Constantinople. Today I bicycle down Caesar Chavez Boulevard in Austin, Texas, and I sometimes eat a Caesar salad. We all know people named Caesar, a common name around the world.

How would the name Caesar Augustus sound to Mary and Joseph as they heard the command to be taxed repeated through their town after its long journey from Rome? Would it have chilled their spines, or caused an eye roll? We do not know. We know so little about people from this time, or really any time in the past. Their inner lives are like the ocean, mysterious and dark, with shifting currents and tides. We also know very little about ourselves in the aftermath of trauma. We have sensations and feelings but are often unsure what to make of them. Some chill our spines, others bore us. And so we imagine this young couple through our post-traumatic lens. They are subject to a distant power who demands they travel for a census so they can be taxed. This distant power has local agents, a complex system of bureaucrats and muscle, papyrus, and iron. If they do not go, they lose everything, maybe even their lives.

One of the emerging areas of trauma research concerns complex post-traumatic stress disorder (C-PTSD). Simply put, this is what people get from being hostages. The inability to exercise bodily autonomy with the threat of death hanging over your head does something to the body, soul, and mind. Even Freud found that the "threat of annihilation" caused signs of a "Daemonic force at work."[1]

Mary and Joseph, as well as the rest of the Jews of their day, were hostages to Rome. They had very little bodily autonomy, and they lived under the threat of death. There are, of course, more extreme examples of being a hostage, but this was their situation. Silently, daily, hourly, the slow drip of trauma released poison into their souls. When this happens, when

human beings are subjected to this kind of slow-drip traumatic
threat, the demonic thrives. We will see in later stories how
many demons inhabited the land, plunging people and animals
into fires and off cliffs. Self-destruction is the only freedom of
the hostage, and the demons whisper, "Do it." The demons
whisper, "Do it, before the other Roman boot falls."

Surely Mary and Joseph knew relatives who tried to trick
Rome or perhaps defy them outright. We know from Josephus
that the whole land was a powder keg of insurrection and tension, and this kind of terror lives in the body. Bessel van der
Kolk's landmark book *The Body Keeps the Score* has become
an essential study for how we understand trauma.[2] Trauma
reorganizes our brain to tell our body that the trauma is still
going on. Therefore every experience we have in our bodies is
contaminated by our trauma. What a wonder, then, to see the
Messiah being miraculously conceived in a body that is keeping the score.

The miracle of the incarnation is staggering in its gran-
deur, and over the centuries Christians have meditated on the
mystery of Mary's body. Many hold to the doctrine of Mary's
immaculate conception, meaning that her mother also conceived *her* without sexual intercourse, on the reasoning that
this would make her born without sin, holy enough to give
birth to God. Even if we reject the immaculate conception and
the sinlessness of Mary for whatever theological reason, we still
honor her for her role in the drama of the world's redemption.
And if we honor her in any way, we must see her as both holy
and traumatized. The one who bears in her body the child who
will end death itself also carries in her body the trauma of being
human. She is truly one of us, and the child she will bear will
be one of us too.

When Mary swaddles the newborn Jesus, she is wrapping
him in the inherited trauma of her people and the inherited
trauma of being human. We wrap babies tightly because we
want them to feel safe again after leaving the safety of the
womb. We want them to feel like they are being embraced,
hugged, and nurtured. We don't want them to be afraid of the

terrors we face. We want them to feel, if only for a moment, what it feels like to be OK. This is what Mary did for Jesus, this is what our mothers have done for us, and this is what we can do for each other.

Birth, by any means, is traumatic for child and mother, and as a male observer of birth, I never cease to be mystified, horrified, and filled with gratitude for my own. There's nothing in my world that could compare to what a mother goes through in those pain-filled hours. Even the babies' brush with death in the birth canal, their scream being the sign of life when they emerge, is the closest thing to death I've seen that wasn't death. Birth is dangerous, even without the threat of soldiers searching for newborn babies to kill.

But this is exactly what happens in the traumatic story of Jesus' birth, as told in the Gospel of Matthew (2:1–16). While we sing "Silent Night," a mad king bellows an order to kill all the children under two years old, to exterminate he who is born King of the Jews.

4
Dreams and Nightmares

When Joseph first learned of Mary's pregnancy, he planned to "dismiss her quietly," Matthew's Gospel says (1:19), because he did not want her to be publicly humiliated or punished. His mind is changed by a dream that speaks to him as only dreams can speak to us in our trauma. "Do not be afraid to take Mary as your wife," an angel says, "for the child conceived in her is from the Holy Spirit" (1:20). Matthew tells us very little else about the remainder of Mary's pregnancy, moving instead to the looming threat of King Herod—but the significance of dreams will be a recurring theme.

When Jesus is born, Herod is in his final days. Like Hitler ranting in his bunker as the Soviet Army rolls into Berlin, so Herod thrashes about as his body begins to fail him. Josephus tells us he colored his gray hair black to appear younger and stronger.[1] He had been strong, once, and young. In his youth he had cut a dashing figure on his horse. Herod, the son of a Nabatean king who had converted to Judaism, rode his cavalry troop hard to rescue none other than Mark Antony from an ambush, thus solidifying the favor of Rome's favorite son. With this favor he rose to power by marrying the stunningly beautiful and connected Mariamne, the granddaughter of the Jewish high priest-king Hyrcanus. To marry Mariamne, he had to banish his first wife, Doris, and his son.

Josephus comments repeatedly on Mariamne's beauty and the beauty of her children. He tells a story of how Herod and Mariamne tried to secure an appointment to the high priesthood for their son by sending portraits of him to Mark Antony, who commented that the boy of sixteen and his siblings were so handsome: "These children seemed not derived from men, but from some God or other."[2] And thus, Mark Antony's lust was kindled to prey on the boy sexually. Herod, realizing this, forbade his son to be violated thusly and made excuses to Mark Antony that the boy could not leave Judea because he was so popular with the people. Mark Antony only held off an attempt at assaulting Mariamne, the boy's mother, because he did not want to anger Cleopatra, his manipulative lover. And so we see that trauma begets trauma, trickling down like sand in an hourglass of pain.

Herod called himself king and did his best to ingratiate himself to Cleopatra and Mark Antony by paying tribute to them and exacting tribute from the king of Arabia. As Mark Antony fought his rivals for control of Rome, Herod fought a proxy war for him against the king of Arabia, whose tribute payments had fallen to a trickle. In his defeat of the Arabians, Herod showed himself to be a holy warrior riding in the cause of justice. In a speech, he spoke of the immorality of the Arabians and how that had angered God. "Now where God is, there is both multitude and courage," he told his troops.[3] Herod performed the Jewish sacrifices before the battle, and his inspired troops beat the Arabs soundly.

But as Herod was slaughtering the Arabs for Mark Antony, Mark Antony had lost to Octavian, who eventually became the emperor Caesar Augustus. But Herod was resourceful and soon won favor with Octavian, partly by supplying him with gladiators to feed the Roman lust for blood in their macabre games. Herod also gathered so many talents of gold that Octavian could not refuse him the crown as king of the Jews.

Every single day of Herod's reign was devoted to eliminating threats to his reign. Mariamne was soon suspected of poisoning him, a detail Herod suspected because she refused to have sex with him. And so he tortured her favorite enslaved eunuch to find the truth. The eunuch knew of no poison plot but did say she was unhappy with some of his decisions. She stood trial and was executed, nobly walking to her death with a calm and resolute face. The death of his wife was said to have distressed the mad king greatly: "For his love to her was not of a calm nature; nor such as we usually meet with among other husbands."[4] He would call for her often and indecently, lamenting her absence. There are accounts that he kept her encased in honey for seven years, desecrating her corpse sexually in what became known as the "deed of Herod."[5] He tried to distract himself with hunting and feasting, but eventually he ended up in solitude, in the desert with a headache in the back of his head. His physicians could not help him, and they gave up their treatment of the grieving, guilt-addled king.

In his self-inflicted grief, Herod doubled down on his massive building campaign, including the Tower of Mariamne in Jerusalem. He also tried to promote his Jewish identity with his subjects by building the magnificent Temple grounds that Jesus walked in and by whose stones Jews still gather to pray at the Western Wall. He also introduced the extravagances of the Greeks and Romans to his people, creating a whole segment of Jewish society called the Herodians.

But in spite of all his great buildings and political achievements, Herod was a vain, paranoid despot and fool, murdering his own son and heir to the throne in the end. The news of Herod's filicide reached Caesar Augustus, who joked that it was better to be Herod's pig than his son, a reference to the fact that Herod would not eat pork as a Jew. (The joke is funnier in the original language, since the Greek words for pig, *huus,* and son, *huios,* sound similar.) Surrounded by Germanic bodyguards while publicly practicing Jewish piety, Herod fit neither in Jerusalem nor Rome.

It is likely that Mary and Joseph would have known all this about Herod, as would everyone in their world. News like this travels fast. There was also resistance to Herod in their community, resistance that Herod crushed mercilessly, even when the threat was imagined. The Jewish factions we meet in the Gospels—Pharisees, Sadducees, Zealots, and Herodians—were largely forged as responses to Herod the Great's personality.

When the magi come to Herod with their astrological calculations that a king of the Jews has been born, his paranoid violence against all boys under two years of age fits with his character. We can see his conniving cruelty in his secret meeting with the magi. That the magi are warned in a dream not to return to Herod for their own safety after they worship the baby shows that even God must work around Herod's sharp cruelty.

Joseph is also warned in a dream to flee to Egypt for safety. Once Herod dies, Joseph and his family return. Why so many dreams of warning in this story? Why did God send so many dreams so that the magi and the Holy Family could avoid Herod's wrath? When we look at the story through a post-traumatic lens, the role of dreams for traumatized people becomes clear.

For so many post-traumatic people, sleep is a place of horror. The traumatized Job mused,

> When I say, "My bed will comfort me,
> my couch will ease my complaint,"
> then you scare me with dreams
> and terrify me with visions,
> so that I would choose strangling
> and death rather than this body.
> I loathe my life; I would not live forever.
> Let me alone, for my days are a breath.
>   Job 7:13–16

"Just as traumatic memories are unlike ordinary memories, traumatic dreams are unlike ordinary dreams," says Judith Herman. In our sleeping state, the filters on our reality are gone and our terrors come to us raw, in fragments of horror—nightmares from which we cannot wake up. Many drink or use other substances to keep their dreams dead and silent, but those dreams have a way of breaking through the film of sleep. "In sleep as well as in waking life," writes Herman, "traumatic memories appear to be based in an altered neurophysiological organization."[6]

That there are so many dreams about Herod shouldn't surprise us. We should expect such a man to produce such dreams and visions. Like Job, Joseph and the magi know that the source of their nightmares is God.

In traumatic events, the thin veil of civilization is torn from top to bottom, and we never see the world the same way again. We see the way God sees, with the knowledge of good and evil, and that knowledge presses in on us even when we sleep and dream. For the magi and Joseph, their trauma has opened this channel to God, and as troubling as the dreams must be, the message is clear: they are not safe.

My mentor, Gulf War veteran and army chaplain Dave Scheider, says, "PTSD is the loss of the illusion of safety." Safety is an illusion, and terrible things can happen at any time. Once something traumatic happens, then we are no longer fooled into assuming we are safe. We have eaten of the tree in the garden and we are like God, knowing good and evil. The terrifying dreams have a message, and we must bring them to God and ask what they mean. We must bring them to our therapists and counselors and ask their meaning, knowing we already understand that the meaning is always some variation of "Get to safety as fast as you can. Herod cannot get you there." *really?*

5

The First Temptation

We can imagine them there, crouching by a small campsite in the desert. Two men eye each other to see who will make the first move. While this is a campsite, there is no food or water here. Just the empty wilderness, hunger, and thirst. As the sun begins to blaze, the two shrink closer to the rock wall. There are rocks everywhere, some jagged, others round. The newcomer to the camp says, "If you are the son of God, command these rocks to become bread."

This is how the showdown begins. The devil—aka El Diablo, the Slanderer—tempts Jesus with a magic trick. But the starving man has already seen magic tricks in the desert. As Luis Alberto Urrea writes in his account of the dehydrating trek from Mexico to the USA on foot, you "see God and devils."[1] Early accounts of desert perils include the loss of sense and reason as desperation increases. The mind grows weak as the brain cooks itself in the skull. At a certain point you cannot bleed, as the blood coagulates. The living bodies of one's companions are looked upon as a source of moisture. Mirages appear ahead, small clouds drift in the sky. A desperate man sucks on the body of a scorpion for the smallest drop.

And so Jesus walks with blistered feet with the millions who have trekked across barren wastelands, their minds and bodies failing them. His cracked lips speak a response: "One does not live by bread alone" (Matt. 4:4). But without food we die, hollow and gaunt, emaciated, desiccated—more mummy than man. And millions have.

The fear of hunger drives us to plow in the thin skin of topsoil that keeps us all alive. We claw and cultivate the earth to grow food, and, if conditions are good, it grows. Our ancestors prayed to the gods and goddesses, in hopes that the warm sun and gentle rains would bless the crops so their children would not starve. Early humans hunted whole species into extinction, and their children continue to attempt this, in spite of our knowledge that once a beast is gone, it is gone forever. Humans fight for food, or for the commodities that make growing food possible. We raid, pillage, and plunder for spoil, taking it home to hungry mouths before it is taken from us. We are afraid of hunger. Even for those of us who never have to wonder from where our next meal will come, a full belly makes us feel safe as darkness falls. Rollo May, in his *The Meaning of Anxiety*, shows how our anxiety can be a "cue to begin eating" and even turn into bulimia for some people.[2] Fear, anxiety, and food are always in a life-and-death dance.

I never struggled with disordered eating until I came home from Iraq. I seemed to be always trying to tamp down my raw anxiety, and binge eating was effective, until it hurt. I was mostly unaware of what I was doing, just acting out my symptoms like the frightened mammal I am. We truly do not know what we do.

But Jesus' answer to the devil is the same answer to our hunger and the disordered ways we express that hunger. We do not live by bread alone, Jesus says, quoting Deuteronomy 8:3, but by every word that comes from God's mouth. And what are the words that come from God's mouth?

During my days of trauma-fueled binge eating, the first therapist I saw answered this question for me. Instead of shaming me for what I was doing, she said, "Every time you take a bite, say, 'I love myself.' Bite, 'I love myself.'" I was floored.

How could I do this? It was so strange to do, but it was God's message to me, that I was loved. The words from God's mouth are always words of love, and they echo down to us through time and space from a desert campsite as we stand over our sink holding an empty box of Girl Scout cookies.

The other two temptations are more esoteric, more abstract. Offering all the kingdoms of the world to Jesus and encouraging a daredevil (no pun intended) plunge off the corner of the Temple seem less immediate than filling a belly that has been starved for forty days and nights. But they are just as tempting to our human longing as a loaf of bread in our anxiety.

Shortly after the colossal Golden Gate Bridge was built in San Francisco, a traumatized World War I veteran named Harry Wobber joined the crowd of people who flocked to walk out onto it. As he stepped off the bus that brought him there, he said to a fellow passenger, "It's a great day, for what I'm going to do."

"What's that?" the passenger asked.

"You'll see," said Wobber.

He walked out to the middle of the bridge, took off his coat, and climbed over the rail. As a man tried to grab his belt he jumped to his death. His body was never found in the strong current.[3]

In the pocket of his discarded coat there was a note to his sixteen-year-old daughter and a day pass from the veterans hospital where he had been treated for combat trauma. Since Wobber's suicide, hundreds more have fallen to their deaths on this bridge and many others around the world.

What voice compelled them to this place? Was it the same voice that spoke to Jesus saying, "Throw yourself down"? We cannot ignore the temptation to suicide after trauma. That has been linked since time immemorial. However, the devil is not compelling Jesus to kill himself; he is tempting him to grandiosity, to be a spectacle, to be a sensation. He is tempting him to save the world by showing how special he is to God, because the angels will catch him. That is a different voice from the one that called Harry Wobber to fall so far so fast.

The next temptation in Matthew has Jesus on a high mountain. Below him all the kingdoms of the world are presented as the reward for worshiping the devil, the false god. The proposal hinges on worship, literally in Greek "to kiss the ground." By bowing his body over into a position of vulnerability and subservience, Jesus will be granted the ultimate invulnerability and power. As van der Kolk has said, in the post-traumatic world our bodies keep the score. We embody our trauma in ways that are as unique as our separate yet connected bodies. How we move our bodies, how we pose them, both voluntarily and involuntary, reflects our wounds and griefs. To have our bodies moved, penetrated, or squeezed in ways we do not like is the very definition of trauma itself. And so this demand by the devil to change Jesus' posture is much more violent than it seems on the surface.

So much of our dis-ease comes from putting our bodies in positions not of our choosing; after trauma, this often results in a violent reaction. The main takeaway from trauma-informed events is to give people an escape, a way out, if they feel the need to escape because their bodies have kept the score. In this encounter on the mountain, Jesus sticks to his original theme—that what the devil wants is not what God wants. What the devil wants to do to Jesus' body is not what Jesus wants to do with his body.

While Jesus counters the first two tests with more nuanced answers, on the mountain he simply screams, "Away with you, Satan!" and then quotes the Scripture that calls us to worship God only and no one else. When the score of our bodies alerts us, we follow the post-traumatic Jesus who blurts his truth out, thus driving the devil away.

The test is over, the angels come. Jesus is fed, loved, and cared for. But the test in the wilderness serves as a reminder to the traumatized that God is on your side and no matter who tries to test you, God will always prevail. The angels will come to you.

6
Come and Die

In 2005, the TV show *Deadliest Catch* showed the world how dangerous it is to fish for Alaskan king crabs. The turbulent sea is a character in the show, tossing the ships and their crews around like snowflakes in a snow globe. In spite of the danger, the catch outweighs the risk. It always does for those who venture out into deep waters.

While the Sea of Galilee is far from the cold Bering Sea, the accounts in the Gospels tell us it was not completely safe. Accounts of storms, leaky boats, and broken nets are presented as everyday risks of fishing these waters—not to mention the ever-present hunger of subsistence fishing, always one torn net away from economic ruin, slavery, and starvation.

This is the life from which Jesus drew his first followers, most notably Peter, Andrew, James, and John. Both Matthew and Mark tell us that they were casting nets into the sea, likely casting nets from shore. The reason the authors give is "because they were fishers." This was their identity, their life. Even with its risks, this is what they did. This is who they were.

The life that Jesus calls them to was much less certain even than fishing. It was a call to a new identity as disciples, followers. These fishers who had been subject to currents, storms, and the migrations of fish now had to subject themselves to the will of another.

This was not easy, or safe, to do. The level of trust this would have required goes far beyond a career switch. The call Jesus issued to Peter, Andrew, James, and John was the call to come and die. Did they know this fully? Probably not. We never do when we follow the call of Jesus. Jesus did indicate in his call to them that the call involves people. They would become fishers of people. People are dangerous, especially when you're "fishing" for them.

The first thing that comes into my head when I hear the term "fishers of men" (in the classic King James Version) is the aggressive style of evangelism that became popular in the twentieth century. I was once a Sunday afternoon door-to-door evangelist, using a fake survey to get people to talk about their faith so I could talk about mine. I did magic tricks to get a crowd in the Philly train stations, then preached that they needed to get saved. This was all before I was twenty. While Jesus' ministry did involve public, outdoor preaching, he was not a Christian evangelical in a suit. Fishing for people was about gathering them around himself so he could heal them, comfort them, and ultimately show them how much God loved them. Whatever it means to be a fisher of people, it ends in death for the fisher, who has given his life for those he has "caught."

Like a film flashback from a deathbed to a first-ever meeting, this scene grew in significance for the Gospel storytellers. They remembered that first moment and likely thought of it often in its powerful simplicity. Together they would face demons, crowds, terror, hunger, panic, betrayal, and the torture and death of their teacher, and it all began in this moment.

How powerful were the details they recalled of their first meeting with Jesus, what they were doing at the time, and then the most important detail—that they left their nets and boats and followed. Jesus calls people to follow him still. The post-traumatic Jesus knows how hard it is to trust, to follow, to have faith that he will be there in the next storm, in the next trial, in the next betrayal, or in the next crucifixion.

The Gospel writers offer us different details of this invitation by the sea in what could be considered an example of "fractured narrative." Tim O'Brien's classic war story *The Things They Carried,* as well as other post-traumatic tales, employ "fractured narrative." The sequence of events jumps around, just as a traumatized person relates the story of their trauma to a police officer or therapist. Traumatic events tear the space-time continuum and make time irrelevant to the discussion. It is as if there is a "time wound" that makes all time flit around, helping our minds avoid the sharp parts until we are exhausted. The fractured narrative of trauma happens in this story, just as it does in so many others in the Gospels. While the accounts in Matthew and Mark are nearly identical, Luke paints a different picture of Peter's calling to be a disciple. In Luke's account, Jesus invites Peter to put his net in the water and—miracle! There is a huge catch of fish! There are so many fish the boat begins to sink, and Peter and his crew must call their colleagues to help collect them all. Peter's immediate response to this miracle is to fall at Jesus' feet, saying, "Go away from me, Lord, for I am a sinful man."

I do not know what Peter means by this self-incriminating disclosure. Luke narrates that he says it because he, and all of the fishers, were amazed by the great catch of fish. It is almost as if Peter is confessing his sinfulness on behalf of all of them. Perhaps we see here not Peter the fisher turned disciple, but Peter the priest, apostle, and bishop, confessing his people's sins and leading them in worship. This is a glimpse of what the three years will do to this man who seems so naive in this first meeting with Jesus. Among the disciples, we see Peter closest, as he is the one the spotlight often focuses upon as he names Jesus as the Messiah, defends Jesus with a concealed blade, and denies he knows him hours before his execution. Peter is the disciple the church knows the most about. In Peter we see ourselves best with all his impulsive exuberance. I certainly see myself in him, even as I attempt to leave my fishing nets of alcohol dependence behind.

Jonathan Shay writes in his *Achilles in Vietnam* that sobriety, the freedom from the drug of alcohol and other substances, is essential for healing from trauma.[1] He should know—he spent a career caring for traumatized veterans from World War II on down. I should know too.

I never drank before my war, and I couldn't stop after it. I'd quit here and there, after some broken ribs from a blackout bike crash or an argument, but go right back to it as soon as my anxiety told me I needed something to slow my brain down. Then I'd drink again until the next quitting time. One therapist helped me understand why I drank by holding up a giant expandable toy in the shape of a ball. He said, with the ball fully extended, "This is your world before PTSD. It's big. After PTSD, you shrink your world down to a safe size." He shrunk the ball to a tiny fraction of its immense potential. Alcohol helps us shrink our world really fast.

The disciples leaving fishing is a lot like leaving alcohol behind. For me it happened abruptly, when I saw the test results that I was killing my liver. Suddenly the "feel good" substance looked like poison, mainly because it was. My grandfather died at fifty-three from an alcohol-hardened liver, and I saw, at forty-five, the writing on the wall. I wish I'd done it sooner, but that is always our wish. For too long I prayed with the preconversion St. Augustine, "Give me chastity, Lord, but not yet." Immediately I found I was able to follow Jesus in a way I couldn't before. Without being able to rely on alcohol to soothe me, I had to turn and ask Jesus to do that. I had to trust him in a way I never had to before.

I don't feel bad about drinking as much as I did. I really couldn't do anything different after what I went through in the war and its aftermath. If anything, I'm surprised I didn't drink more. Shame doesn't give freedom, only more entanglement. Freedom is found in leaving and following. The same Jesus that called Peter and company calls you and me, and the demand is the same: Come and die, so that you may come and live. Yes, is our answer.

7

Healing Dis-ease

Jesus lived in the period of time referred to as the "Roman Climate Optimum" (RCO), a period of human history "marked by stability, warmth, and precipitation."[1] This relatively brief period (200 BC to AD 150) of favorable weather produced an abundance of crops and conditions for the expansion of Rome and thereby everyone else in the Roman world. As abundant harvests continued year after year, populations grew. With that growth, microscopic horrors began to take their place on the world stage.

The first pandemic, a world-encompassing disease that spread uncontrollably, was the Antonine Plague, named after the Roman emperor who presided over the devastation in AD 165, well after Jesus walked on the earth. In Jesus' day there were epidemics, local outbreaks of deadly diseases. In time, these diseases would bring an empire to its knees. Local outbreaks were treated with brutally enforced quarantines and prayers to the gods and goddesses at hand. Apollo was a popular object of plague-abatement devotion. But the tiny agents of misery moved at the speed of human travel and connection. Smallpox has an incubation period of seven to nineteen days, a false lull, in which the host is not contagious or symptomatic but can travel great distances; thus, the disease can pop up in a new town or city. Merchants, soldiers, refugees, and diplomats spread diseases along the well-built Roman roads at a speed never before achieved.

Smallpox, the likely disease of the Antonine Plague, killed indiscriminately and left survivors maimed and blind, orphaned and alone. Surviving children were often sold into slavery, thus adding to the misery of the times.

While people in Jesus' day did not have microscopes and what we now call "germ theory," they were not fools. They knew plagues were passed from person to person. Leviticus 13 goes into great detail about what leprosy looked like and the symptoms accompanying it. While it is not clear if the modern disease we call leprosy, Hansen's disease, was, in fact, the disease mentioned in Leviticus and in the Gospels, the treatment is physical separation from the uninfected. "The person who has the leprous disease shall wear torn clothes and let the hair of his head be disheveled; and he shall cover his upper lip and cry out, 'Unclean, unclean.' He shall remain unclean as long as he has the disease; he is unclean. He shall live alone; his dwelling shall be outside the camp" (Lev. 13:45–46). Masks, isolation, and stigma were the lifelong lot of lepers.

Romans invoked Apollo for help during plagues. One inscription reads, "Woe! Woe! A powerful disaster leaps onto the plain, a pestilence hard to escape from, in one hand wielding a sword of vengeance, and in the other lifting up the deeply mournful images of mortals newly stricken. In all ways it distresses the new-born ground which is given over to Death—and every generation perishes—and headlong tormenting men it ravages them."[2] One amulet found in Roman London forbade kissing, kissing being the standard greeting of the day in the Roman world of Jesus.[3] Fumigation of buildings was also practiced to ward off plague, a treatment originally propagated by the famous Hippocrates.

Given the biblical instructions regarding leprosy, it would not be surprising that many diseases in Jesus' day would fall under that category, and the isolating treatment would be the same. We can see her now, a young woman feeling the pustules grow in her throat, the black bile cough described by the ancient physician Galen. Her horror and dread grows as word spreads of others with symptoms, then weak good-byes and death. There is pain, there is loneliness, as caregivers succumb to the disease. The crops lie in the field. The farm animals wander off. For the survivors there are traumatic wounds of the soul to accompany their disfigured faces. There is an impending sense of doom. The world is ending.

Matthew's Gospel summarizes Jesus' early ministry in this way:

> Jesus went throughout Galilee, teaching in their synagogues and proclaiming the good news of the kingdom and curing every disease and every sickness among the people. So his fame spread throughout all Syria, and they brought to him all the sick, those who were afflicted with various diseases and pains, demoniacs, epileptics, and paralytics, and he cured them. (Matt. 4:23–24)

His preaching is intimately connected to the diseases he's healing. The first word above for "disease" is the same word used in the Septuagint (the Greek translation of the Hebrew Bible) for the plagues of Egypt. The other word translated "sickness" here is literally "softness," an inability to be strong and virile. It is a form of the word used in other contexts for effeminate, "soft" men in the New Testament (1 Cor. 6:9). There is a moral tone in these words we cannot miss.

All disease is moral, even viruses. The COVID-19 pandemic is loaded with moral implications, even in our scientific age. When people take precautions and get it, there is a sense of shame and failure. When unvaccinated people contract the disease and die, their pictures are shared online to be mocked by thousands.

When we stare into the mirror and know we have a failing liver, HIV, or a sexually transmitted infection (STI), we feel the moral tone of the disease. We have failed in some way, and our disease is proof of that. We cannot disconnect our morality from our epidemiology no matter how hard we try. And this makes all disease worse, as it always has. The psychological effects of this sometimes equal the debilitation of the disease, especially with STIs.

Unclean! Unclean! We hear the voice shout. Even the language of addiction uses this religious language: "I've been clean for five months." We are always living in the past, with its shadows and dread. What sacrifices we would perform to be clean again.

Matthew's list of those "afflicted" (also translated "hard-pressed") goes on. Is this the post-traumatic signature, that impending doom and dread, the inability to see good things ahead, blue skies, the love of friends? St. Paul said he was "hard-pressed" on every side, in anguish over threats to his life and freedom. "Pains" (Matt. 4:24) is the strangest Greek term of the lot. It literally means "touchstone," a stone often called a "Lydian stone" that, when rubbed on pure gold, would make a specific mark indicating it was indeed the real thing. If a person were to be examined this way, it would be torturous—scraped like a tax collector scrapes a gold coin with a Lydian stone. These people were "tortured" as only an affliction can torture. This is the word used in the story of Lazarus and the rich man, who called the Hades of his tormenting "this place of pains." The people coming to Jesus were in hell on earth, a living torment, a hopeless prison.

The next word, "demoniacs," fits snugly in this list of maladies in a way it would not in the modern world. Whether the demons controlling this group are external personal spiritual entities or metaphors for mental illness does not matter much. The torment is the same for the victim.

Then there are the epileptics. The Greek here is literally "moonstruck," transforming into the English "lunatic." Luna, the moon, pulls us into madness and fear. The psalmist invokes this moon madness with, "The sun shall not smite thee by day, nor the moon by night" (Ps. 121:6 KJV). How can the moon strike? Only those who have been struck know. The paranoia, the lashing out, the dread and fear—it possesses the whole soul, and no amount of talking down or love will cure it. All we can do is howl, often silently.

Then there are the *paralytics*, a Greek word we have borrowed directly in English. Literally, it means to be loose on one side, perhaps alluding to the main symptom of palsy, stroke, or some other source of damage to the nerves on one side of the body. Paralytics were immobilized, dependent on the charity and strength of others. Jesus meets many who suffer from this who get up and walk, to great amazement. How many were made so by trauma and how many by genetics or by diseases they survived?

This list of patients in a single hospital hallway would astound us with their stories of loss, both gradual and sudden. Even today modern physicians could likely not cure all of them, but if they could, there would still be the hidden wounds that lie beneath.

Jesus becomes popular with the masses of all Syria (Rome's name for the whole region along the eastern edge of the Mediterranean) because he gets close to these people. He is announcing the dawning of a new age, and these miracles are signs of that new age of God's reign. It is comforting to me to think of this—that the sign of God's presence in a place is the healing of these conditions that are often connected to shame and dis-ease.

The incarnation of God in Jesus Christ is the simple message that God cares. This is hard to see through the lens of our trauma. In our post-traumatic condition we must stop caring because it hurts so bad, wrenching our hearts into a bloody pulp. We must turn our hearts to stone, or make them numb with chemicals or cruelty. We cannot face the reality that we might be loved, cared for, noticed.

But this is the message of Jesus' life, and there he is, at the edge of our village. We stumble to him with these others, bad company in any other time but good company when he is here.

8

The Beatitudes:
A Trauma Manifesto

Without our post-traumatic lens, the Sermon on the Mount should be called the Serum on the Mount or the Cliché on the Mount. Reading Jesus' words in Matthew 5:1–11 (similar to those in Luke 6:17–26) from an air-conditioned apartment in the 2020s makes the sermon sound like good advice from a motivational speaker trying to enhance your performance, in the boardroom or in the bedroom. *Be humble! Be sensitive! You'll thank me for this!* No, for traumatized people these words meet us where we are.

"Blessed are the poor in spirit, for theirs is the kingdom of heaven" only resonates with those who are already poor in spirit. Jesus is not calling for a mood dump or for comfortable followers to get poor. He is not calling for us to go on a silent retreat or ladle potato salad at the shelter. No, Jesus' listeners already are poor in spirit, beaten down by the systemic oppression of Rome and the internal poverty of an absent God. Poverty of spirit, the empty spiritual bank account, comes from having it beaten out of us. We know we are poor in spirit when we wander out into the dark night, stare at the silent stars, and whisper, "Fuck you, man," because we cannot summon the

breath to shout it. It is Job, this close to cursing God and dying.
If we had the strength to accuse God with force we would do
it, but we cannot. All we can do is weep when we think of how
short the child's life was, or how we should have known better.

"Blessed are those who mourn, for they shall be comforted."
Again, Jesus is not saying everyone should take up their mourn-
ing clothes and start wailing; his listeners already are.

"Blessed are the meek, for they shall inherit the earth." The
offer the devil made to Jesus in his temptation was just this, but
by another way. Bow down and worship me, he said, and you
shall inherit the earth. No, the meekness here is the downcast
eyes of the victims, who have no control of their bodily integ-
rity. They await another strike, another blow, another wound.
This is not a strong man being humble; this is all humanity
buckled and crumpled at the feet of overwhelming pain. The
meek cannot inherit anything; they can only lose a little more.

Those who hunger and thirst for righteousness will be filled.
They are merciful, they will receive mercy. They are pure in
heart, they will see God. What is good and holy in them is
forged in fire, in the crucible of existence on a planet that
shows no mercy. Those who are persecuted for righteousness'
sake have looked into the abyss, and the abyss has looked back
into them. They have seen the horror, the shock, the awe, the
banality of evil. They no longer have illusions about things
progressing, getting better, turning out right in the end. All
they have is God, a post-traumatic God who is revealed in the
humanity of God's post-traumatic son, who is down here in
the shit with us.

The Sermon on the Mount is not aspirational; it does not
set an agenda or a new code of conduct to make us behave better. The Sermon on the Mount simply describes what it looks
like to follow a post-traumatic Jesus. Ultimately, Christians
follow a person, and that person bears in his body the marks of
his trauma. This does not mean we must suffer trauma to follow Jesus. All of us suffer from the trauma of the world, either
firsthand or secondhand, and so we best understand his teachings through that post-traumatic lens.

The final line of Jesus' introductory poem is "Blessed are you when people revile you, persecute you, and utter all kinds of evil against you falsely on my account." This is exactly what happens to Jesus in the final days of his life. As he hangs between earth and sky, his enemies spit on him, mocking his powerlessness. He is, by every definition, persecuted. The Greek word translated "persecute" literally means to chase, to pursue. Perhaps "hounded" or "hunted" fits the context here. As Jesus' followers hide in latrines in hopes their pursuers pass them by for the stench, they experience this blessing. After all, Jesus knows what he's talking about. No doubt his mother told him about being hunted by Herod in his infancy.

Narratives of being hunted abound in the biographies of the traumatized warlords of the earth. Temuchin, better known as Genghis Khan, was hunted by his enemies as child. His harrowing escape forged in him a steely revenge he exacted in the blood of his pursuers when he finally came of age. But the hunted Christmas child takes a different path. He loves his enemies and boldly declares his followers will do this too. His love flows not from a charmed childhood, but from a violent one. The life he calls us to has no illusions of safety or tranquility. His invitation is to come and die.

While the Sermon on the Mount covers a wide range of situations and topics—everything from divorce to what names not to call your brother—my post-traumatic vision hones in on how to deal with an enemy (Matt. 5:38–48).

Jesus starts with the *lex talionis*, the ancient rule of an eye for an eye, a tooth for a tooth. This is the law of the jungle, the law of the cave, the law of the street fight. This law is as ancient as the gash, cut, or murder. It is the essence of justice, a way of limiting the violence of revenge and retribution. Without this law, the cycle of violence would continue with blood feud after blood feud, and there would be no one left alive. Even with this law on the books for all time and eternity, it has done very little to stem the tide of human retribution.

As Miroslav Volf writes, when a wrong has been done, there are three responses. There is revenge, the disproportionate response to evil; justice, the proportionate response to evil; and forgiveness, which is a gift of something entirely different.[1] Jesus' teachings are practical: Do not resist an evildoer. If someone strikes you on the right cheek, turn your left so he can hit you again. If anyone wants your coat, give him your cloak too. If someone forces you to march one mile, go the second mile (vv. 39–41).

Jesus' very matter-of-fact commands on how to act in these situations float above the murky surface of trauma and evil. Who could do these things to us but a madman, a tyrant, an abuser? Who but a monster would strike you a second time once you let your guard down? Who would take your clothes and leave you standing there naked and shivering? Who would force you to march with them on a hard road for a mile? The obvious answer is a Roman soldier.

"I am a man under authority," says one Roman soldier to Jesus (Luke 7:8 // Matt. 8:9). Roman soldiers in Palestine were subject to strict orders when it came to how they dealt with the civilian population. Many of the soldiers who occupied the world of Jesus were likely from nearby Syria and hated Jewish people.[2] However, the abuse had to be subtle and nonlethal. Like all abuse, it had to fit neatly into what the law allowed, which is not to say it was not abuse. So much evil has been perfectly within the bounds of the law, and humanity bears the scars.

A backhand strike, the only way for a right-handed person to strike you on your *right* cheek, is what some call the "pimp slap" or the "bitch slap." It is someone with power hitting someone without any. It is the prison guard hitting the prisoner. To turn the other cheek in this situation happens because we do what Jesus did. While Jesus' sermon is couched in the language of command, his opening poem points to the reality that his followers will act this way, his way, whether anyone tells them to or not. The Beatitudes are in our bones, our flesh, and our wounds.

By turning the other cheek, the abused says, "Hit me like an equal." There is no way to stop the strike, but there is a way to show how empty the power of evil is. This is that way. Jesus is not blessing abuse or urging battered partners to stay in their marriage. He is describing what his followers will do when the shit hits the fan and they are pinioned to their cross.

The others follow the same logic. You cannot prevent an abuser from taking your coat, but when you give him your tunic and stand there naked, who looks ridiculous? Is it the naked man or the man holding his clothing in a bundle? The nakedness of the victim is transformed into a billboard pointing to the injustice, and thereby the power shifts back to the victim.

As the Roman soldier compels the peasant to carry his pack for a mile, he thinks he has the upper hand. But when the peasant insists on going the second mile with his burden, the Roman army pack becomes the peasant's possession. The soldier now grows anxious, grabbing at his pack and insisting the peasant release it so he can carry on.

Jesus does not offer us systematic solutions to the all-too-human problem of abusive violence, and this is not his telling victims of domestic violence to stay with their abuser and suffer and die. He is describing the kind of bravery his followers will show the world because they follow him. In a few short years the teacher will teach the ultimate lesson from his cross. He will show that although evil has the power to literally nail you to a piece of wood, evil never gets the last laugh. The last laugh goes to the one who knocks the soldiers over as he bursts from his stone-cold tomb.

9

The Traumatized Samaritan

One of the few things we know about the young Herod is that he effectively subdued bandits, gangs of men who preyed upon travelers. At least, people who liked him said he did. Josephus records that at age fifteen, Herod defeated a band of robbers led by a captain named Hezekias. The people of the area were so thankful they composed songs about Herod's victory and sang them in all the towns and villages.[1] Subduing banditry was a major concern of all leaders of the time, and a common theme among those praising those leaders. Velleius Paterculus, who served as an army officer and senator under Augustus and Tiberius, named the era Jesus lived in the "Pax Augusta," for his old boss. He said, "The Pax Augusta, which has spread to the regions of the east and of the west and to the bounds of the north and of the south, preserves every corner of the world safe from the fear of brigandage."[2]

But his boast is pure propaganda. No ruler of the time was all that effective against this scourge of the empire. Bandits harassed the Roman world and were the main threat to the so-called Pax Romana, the era of Roman peace Jesus was born into. Like mass shootings today, the feeling that it could happen at any time had a disproportionate effect on the people living in the Roman world. If it hasn't happened to you, it has probably happened to someone you know. A whole Roman legion was stationed in Spain for centuries, despite the empire having no enemies to its west (due to the Atlantic Ocean). They were kept there because it's easy to hide in Spain if you're a bandit—so too in the caves and wilderness of Judea.

Jesus and his followers were themselves frequent travelers on the dangerous roads of Roman Judea and Galilee. Jesus ventured into the area of Tyre and Sidon, prosperous cities and thus big targets for these men without consciences. His admonition to his followers to "take no staff" for their missional journeys meant they were going into the wild unarmed. Being attacked and robbed by bandits was unpredictable, like all traumatic events. Sometimes women were raped, other times they were not. There is sometimes honor among thieves, we can suppose. There is one curious case of a Jewish man who was a Nazirite, a man who had taken a vow to never cut his hair. This Nazirite fell among thieves, and they shaved his head. Was this to promote fear, to intimate, or just for laughs? Who can know the mind of the bandit?

In the parable Jesus tells, the bandits leave their victim for dead. They beat him. Did they use their hands, sticks, rocks, or cut him with weapons of war until he was a quivering, barely breathing, carcass of wasted humanity? What perverse delight did they get from this? They had his money and his possessions, and he could no longer fight back. We can stare into this murky hole of why, and no answers will emerge. Or, if answers do, they will be unsatisfactory for our emotional need. Were these bandits economically and socially disadvantaged men in need of food and money? A system that excludes certain groups of people drives people to make their living this way, outside the law. Were they driven by mental illness, demons, scarcity, politics? The man left for dead in this story does not care. The wounds are the same no matter the reason they were given.

The indifference of the priest and the Levite who pass him by adds a layer of betrayal to his pain. God has turned his back on this dying man, and now who will come to his aid? He stares at the sky and the circling vultures. They have babies to feed too. He surrenders himself to the thirsty agony of dying slowly and fully aware. He calls on the God who has passed him by and then to his mother, who might just hear him as she did that day when he fell by the sheep pen and called out. She came and scooped up his three-year-old body and all was well.

The surrender to one's own death is an attempt to soothe oneself while dying. A rape survivor describes her experience of this state of surrender: "Did you ever see a rabbit stuck in the glare of your headlights when you were going down a road at night? Transfixed—like it knew it was going to get it—that's what happened." In the words of another rape survivor, "I couldn't scream. I couldn't move. I was paralyzed . . . like a rag doll."[3] After hyperarousal and the intrusion of traumatic memories, Herman names this as the third cardinal symptom of PTSD: constriction.[4] This man who falls among thieves is numb, constricted, left for dead.

And then he sees a face. It is the face of a Samaritan, who puts pressure dressings on his wounds to stop the bleeding. The Samaritan hauls the man's near-dead carcass to an inn, where he gets the best care. His life is saved by a stranger—even an enemy.

Luke uses two Greek words for "wound" in this parable: *plagus* and *trauma*. First, the robbers inflicted *plagus* on the man. *Plagus* is translated as "plague" in Revelation, giving us the English word we still use today for a massive disease that often feels like God's judgment. After the robbers wound him, the Samaritan wraps up his wounds (Greek: *trauma*) in love and care.

Trauma can cause constriction, and we feel we are left for dead like this man was. We may lose hope when we consider how grave our wounds are and how there is little anyone can do to help us. From this story we can learn to trust that help may come from an unlikely source. For this traumatized victim, help came from an enemy, who wrapped his trauma in love.

10

Post-Traumatic Invitation to "Take Up Your Cross"

Reflecting on his service in the trenches in World War I, C. S. Lewis wrote a poem that speaks of his transformation of man to wolf: "Our throats can bark for slaughter: cannot sing."[1]

I am no longer the person who went to war. How could I ever be? Trauma shatters our reality, our identity. We are dehumanized in trauma, our names replaced with numbers or diagnoses. The most extreme examples of this are the tattoos of the people consumed in the Nazi Holocaust, a simple, practical witness to the unnamed horrors of the wholly monstrous.

Traumatized people report this loss of identity so often it is cliché, the opening and plot of most action movies. The protagonist is living a quiet life until the villain kills their loved one. The character is then transformed by revenge. Judith Herman writes, "All the psychological structures of the self—the image of the body, the internalized images of others, and the values and ideals that lend a person a sense of coherence and purpose—have been invaded and systematically broken down."[2] We seek to return to the old identity, pick up where we left off, and we look down and see a pulverized heart, amputated limbs, broken fingers.

We sometimes lose God too. In trauma, as we cry out for help from human and divine sources, the silence of God changes how we think of God. Elie Wiesel, a Holocaust survivor, writes about this in *Night:*

> Never shall I forget those flames which consumed my faith forever. Never shall I forget that nocturnal silence which deprived me, for all eternity, of the desire to live. Never shall I forget those moments which murdered my God and my soul and turned my dreams to dust. Never shall I forget those things, even if I am condemned to live as long as God Himself. Never.[3]

In trauma there is forged for us a post-traumatic identity, with only shadows and echoes of our formal self. And so we stagger around like ghosts, seeing a new identity, a new home, a new God.

When Jesus calls his disciples out to decide on his identity, forcing them to declare to him who they think he is, it is inextricably linked to his crucifixion, just as our identities are inextricably linked to our trauma. In Mark 8 Peter makes this declaration at the Roman city of Caesarea Philippi, itself a monumental announcement of the new identity forced on the world of Jesus. The city had hosted a shrine to Pan, a goat-footed Greek deity who is best known for his pipes and his propensity to sow panic (*Pan-ic*) in soldiers during a battle.

Once Peter declares Jesus is the Messiah, Jesus begins to teach the disciples about the great suffering he will endure, his rejection, and his murder. He also tells them he will rise from the dead in three days. It is as if the shadow of his crucifixion hangs over him now, especially close with this declaration of his identity as the Messiah.

He will be the suffering Messiah, the rejected Messiah, the murdered Messiah. His identity can never be separated from these experiences. And neither can ours, no matter who tries to force us into an identity we can never return to.

Peter tries to do this to Jesus. Immediately after Jesus links his identity with his trauma, Peter takes him aside and rebukes him. The comedy of this moment is not lost on the narrator. The audacity, the nerve, the inability to read the room is palpable. I can hear the early Christians chortling at this part, many of them having met Peter or at least heard anecdotes about him. We might chuckle too from our safe distance. But the public rebuke of Jesus stops the laughter immediately. "Get behind me, Satan," Jesus bellows at Peter, "for you are setting your mind not on divine things but on human things" (Mark 8:33).

It is indeed a very human thing to suffer, to be rejected, to get murdered by the state (but maybe not so much to come back to life in three days). I suspect Peter's rebuke of Jesus centered on Jesus' intention to go to Jerusalem, into the yawning mouth of suffering and abuse. What good friend would not speak a word of caution in a time like this? This is what human friends do. And yet it is in this very human way that Satan speaks through the helpful disciple. How much of our words of wisdom, advice, or help are just the devil's whisper? _ DARK.'

The devil whispers to us that our trauma has nothing to do with our identity. We should get over it and stop making such a big deal. We shouldn't write books about it, for sure, right? But Jesus' rebuke is a rebuke to all well-wishers, positive thinkers, and optimists who seek to divorce us from our post-traumatic identities. I hope this book keeps us from doing this to others. I hope this book keeps me from doing this to myself.

Once the satanic source of Peter's "good advice" is identified, Jesus tells his followers, "If any want to become my followers, let them deny themselves and take up their cross and follow me. For those who want to save their life will lose it, and those who lose their life for my sake, and for the sake of the gospel, will save it" (Mark 8:34–35). Self-preservation is the deepest need of our animal beings. Babies have it the minute they emerge. They have perfected the art of survival before they can open their eyes, and it continues as they grow and develop. Our social anxieties are latent by-products of our drive to survive—not just for our individual selves but for the genetic part of us that lives on. If we are rejected by a potential mate, our offspring will not exist.

It is important to note that Jesus' suffering and death is voluntary, unlike most of our traumatic experiences. And while Jesus enters his trauma willingly, it is still traumatic in that he loses his bodily autonomy after that first step toward Jerusalem. His wounds—physical, spiritual, emotional, mental, and all the places in between these categories that bleed into each other with every crack of the whip and every hammer blow on a nail—are still traumatic.

Jesus' call for his followers to take up their cross and follow him to Golgotha is macabre, grotesque, and insane by any standards. It can only be understood by the post-traumatic soul who sees this path as the ultimate freedom. The inability to escape is the hallmark of trauma, so by walking this path, cross on shoulder, we find the ultimate escape. The path that Jesus lays out for us here—suffering, rejection, death, and resurrection—is the path of all our lives as we walk with him. Rather than rejecting that path, our embrace of it, with Jesus, is the path to real freedom.

This pattern is woven into our stories of hope, our dramas, our comedies. In films and books we see the protagonist suffer, fail, and die either metaphorically or literally. And then there is the resolution, the resurrection. There is also the restoration of the identity lost in trauma. Sometimes it is metaphorical, sometimes literal, but we don't say it was a good story unless it happens. So it is in the story of our lives. We suffer and we die; only then can we be resurrected. This is why so many have looked to the cross for post-traumatic hope. The story Jesus tells about his future suffering, death, and resurrection is the story of all of us, the pattern of our human existence in union with him.

And we are all somewhere in this pattern today. All the stages are difficult, even resurrection, for resurrection leads to labor, advocacy, intercession. We are resurrected to serve others in love, to help them through their suffering, rejection, and death. Our new, post-traumatic identity in Jesus is the credential for this work in the world.

11

The Unmerciful Slave

The institution of slavery is monstrous to behold, in all its forms throughout history and in the present day. Attuned as many American readers are to the horrors of chattel slavery in the New World, we sometimes gloss over the ubiquity of slavery in the world of Jesus. The word translated "slave" or "servant" is *doulos* in Greek. Today this word exists in English as "doula"—a birth, and sometimes death, assistant. Attempts to clean up the Greek word *doulos* as "servant" have been unsuccessful. The slaves in Jesus' life were not from Downton Abbey but the Roman meat grinder. Slavery predated the Romans, but the Romans perfected it, glutting the market and driving down prices with each new conquest.

We can imagine early followers of Jesus, many of them enslaved people, hearing Jesus' parables about slaves and masters told again and again. They did not need to do the work of imagination we must do to enter the parable's world. They lived in it.

How many of them as children would have been separated from their parents and sold by a moody and capricious master? How many would have been beaten with many stripes like the slaves in Jesus' parable? What is abstract to us was concrete to them, sealed in the memory of their bodies. Thus, these parables with enslaved people likely provoked long buried memories, bringing symptoms of trauma to the surface.

In her groundbreaking book *Post-Traumatic Slave Syndrome*, Joy DeGruy argues that the embodied effects of slavery still hold onto Black Americans in ways they often don't fully realize. The self-destruction, violence, and internalized racism she describes still benefit white Americans, creating opportunities for exploitation and discrimination. We can imagine that the multigenerationally enslaved people in Jesus' world carried similar wounds, wounds that might be exposed in a story about a slave and his family. I imagine this as a white man, fully privileged to be part of the group benefiting from the legacy of enslavement of my fellow Americans. And so I must read these parables through the eyes of the enslavers as much as the other characters in the story.

The story is known as the parable of the Unjust Servant or the Wicked Servant, a spoiler coming down to us from those who named it. In 1528 William Tyndale called it the parable of the Wicked Mammon. In context this parable is an answer to Peter's question "Lord, if another member of the church sins against me, how often should I forgive? As many as seven times?" (Matt. 18:21).

The main character in the story is someone who can owe money to a king, so it is clear he is not enslaved in the way we think of slavery today. In the Roman world, a public toilet might be emptied by a free man, while your physician might be enslaved. The threat that hangs over his head is the threat of his wife and children being sold into slavery. He can see the horror of this moment vividly, and the anticipation of horror is in itself traumatizing.

The enslaved man owes an inordinate amount of gold to the king. It is a debt he could never pay with his labor. There is only one way to pay: with his body. Torture, imprisonment, execution, and the horror his mind darts to but then darts away from—his wife and children being sold on the block to the richest letch in the market. He is desperate, in need, helpless really. In his despair he cries out to the king for mercy. The story is extreme, like all the parables. They are meant to hold our attention, and they still do. They exist in the plausible yet implausible world of trauma. Brutal, nasty, and short are the lives of the players, and the losers get tortured or die. So his cry is intense, primal, visceral, bloodcurdling, as only the damned can cry. It is his eleventh hour, the only hour when we cry out like this.

But the king, for whatever reason, pardons him. The king forgives his debt completely and the man is free to go. White Americans like me have little sense that anyone could have this kind of power over us. We trust that if we follow the rule of law and are (relatively) polite to police, the system will work for us. Black Americans, and other people of color, do not have this privilege. There are many kinglike figures in their lives that can determine their fate in a second. Jesus' audience included people who understood this innately. Jesus himself was killed by a last-minute decision made by an aloof ruler.

And yet in our parable the king is God. This would have been obvious to the original hearers as well as most people who read or heard this story throughout history. It is only in a privileged age that some have made the king the evil one. The king's generosity does not prompt love, harmony, and peace in the forgiven debtor. He goes into the street, where he encounters a fellow slave who owes him a small, reasonable sum—almost pocket change compared to the immense debt that was just forgiven. But instead of a normal human reaction to share the wealth, share the forgiveness ("Drinks are on me, boys!"), he does the opposite. When the slave cannot pay on the spot, the forgiven slave begins to choke him mercilessly. The torture he dreaded for himself he metes out upon the neck of his comrade.

To be choked to death is the most intimate form of murder humans can do to each other. Like Judas's kiss, it points to the relationship, the trust, the vile rage that lurks in the human heart. The small bones in the neck are fragile, and our windpipes can only take so much pressure from thumbs and fingers.

Police departments have banned chokeholds, wherein the airway is restricted, but people still die from choking by police. George Floyd's death by choking gave the world his last words:

> Sir
>
> Please
>
> I cannot breathe [at least sixteen times]
>
> Water
>
> Mama
>
> Don't kill me . . . I'm about to die . . .
>
> Everything hurts . . . Mama

And the teller of this parable is asphyxiated on the cross, choked by the hands of the whole world. *Everything hurts, Mama, Mother Mary. . . .*

But just as a young woman filmed George Floyd's death, so it was that many saw this forgiven slave choking his peer in the street. They went to the king, and the king called him in and sent him to be tortured until he paid his impossibly large debt—in other words, forever.

It is in this parable we see the power of post-traumatic prayer. Those who witnessed this choking were horrified. Perhaps some did what we all do, stare in disbelief and call it surreal. It all happened so fast. And then they went to the king. And so do we when we witness the injustices of the world. And the king hears and acts.

Of all the parables, this one tells a traumatized world that God listens when we cry out. In fact, in this parable it seems as if God listens more attentively than he does at the asphyxiation of his own son on the cross. Justice is done, in the end, but it is done by God, not us.

Forgiveness in this parable is like a Rube Goldberg machine—mechanical, precise, exacting. Each little ball of forgiveness we give rolls down the channel and knocks the dominoes over until the final forgiveness of God comes back around. If you don't forgive your brother from your heart, all this bad stuff will happen to you. It's simplistic for a reason. Traumatized people need simple mechanisms to keep alive.

One of my jobs in Iraq was to be part of a team that did debriefings for solders who had, just hours before, lost one of their comrades on the battlefield. Most of these were vehicle explosions from the enemies' well-placed improvised explosive devices (IEDs). One of my colleagues, a psychiatrist, would often tell a soldier at the end of such a debriefing, "I want you to think of one purpose you have to keep going—just one thing that will keep you going." He said this because those soldiers would have to go back out the next day and face the same enemy. They needed things to be simple to survive. I think of them when I read this parable. When you've been through the things enslaved people have been through, when you have been through the traumas of Jesus' world and ours, simple steps are survival steps.

This parable is not the final theology on forgiveness. There is much more to say, of course. However, there is enough in this parable to get you through the rest of the day. There is enough here to survive.

Jesus taught us to pray with the line, "Give us today our daily bread. And forgive us our debts, as we also have forgiven our debtors" (Matt. 6:11–12). Daily bread and forgiveness are linked in some way, just as our forgiveness of others is linked to God's forgiveness of us. Just enough bread for today, please God. Just enough forgiveness for today.

12

Are Women Human?

While the Roman general (later emperor) Vespasian was conquering Judea in the Jewish War, he took an excursion to see the famous Dead Sea, the lowest spot on earth. It is a lake with no outlet, and so the water that pours in every day simply evaporates, thus increasing the salt and mineral content. It was here that the cruel Roman selected prisoners who could not swim, tied them hand and foot, and threw them into the lake in a macabre experiment. They popped to the surface and survived.[1]

In Jesus' day this body of water was known as Asphalt Lake for the blobs of asphalt or bitumen that floated in it. Josephus described these floating petroleum seepages as being like giant black bull carcasses with no heads. The black sludge had many uses, from medicine to home repair, and thus it was harvested like any commodity in their time or ours. The job was tricky, as the substance would adhere to one's boat. All this is described by Josephus, who delighted in these kinds of details. But then Josephus says something strange. He says that the harvesters used menstrual blood to detach the globules of bitumen clinging to the sides of the boat. They also used urine, which would seem to have been more readily available. But Josephus's reference to menstrual blood here, as if it had magical properties, points to a deeper attitude toward women that we encounter numerous places in the world of Jesus: that women are not really human. At least, they are not really human the way men are human.

The law of Moses declares menstruating women ritually unclean, since they were literally shedding blood, just as a warrior was unclean while shedding blood on the battlefield. The blood shed by women is timed with the moon, a heavenly body from which we get our words "lunatic" and "lunacy." To be a woman in Jesus' day, as it is in ours, was inherently traumatic, and it was made more so because women were never believed.

Trauma research emerged from studying hysteria in women. After interviewing "hysterical" women, Freud pointed out that they were repressing memories of traumatic sexual assaults in their childhood. Freud eventually named the talking about these experiences psychoanalysis, and a new field of knowledge was born. His research led him to conclude that the respectable, genteel society of Vienna was rife with horrific sexual predation on children. This realization troubled Freud. Could this seemingly orderly society be so rapacious and cruel? Could it be possible? Faced with this dilemma, Freud stopped listening to women, essentially ignoring their trauma narratives and twisting their words to fit his narrative. This can be seen in his cruel treatment of the hysterical patient Dora.

Dora was sexually abused by many men, all of these encounters facilitated by her father. But instead of validating her feelings of outrage and humiliation as he had done with other patients before her, Freud doubled down on her erotic experiences, trying to convince her that she had invited her abuse as some sort of wish fulfillment. Outraged and humiliated even further, Dora quit the treatment. This shift in Freud was a shift in belief that traumatized victims beyond what their original trauma had done.[2] To not be believed is the cruelest insult.

And so it has always gone. What were you wearing that night? How drunk were you? You went to his hotel room?

What were you thinking? So you wanted it to happen? With unbelief we inflict trauma upon trauma, wound upon wound, cruelty upon cruelty. We can fit abuse and trauma into our moral universe, but we cannot fit betrayal into it. When those who love us tell us we are liars, there is no healing, no relief.

Are women human? Or are they magical creatures who give us pleasure, bear children, and annoy us with their complaints? This question is at play in Jesus' intersections with women in the Gospels, and the shadows of trauma are never out of the picture.

When Jesus meets a woman who has a hemorrhage that has lasted for twelve years, he meets her in this world—a world where no one believes her, a world where her blood cries out but no one listens.

While Matthew, Mark, and Luke record this story, Mark, the sparest and shortest Gospel, has the longest account. Mark tells us that the woman had consulted many physicians but that they had only made her worse. Luke, a physician himself, simply says that "no one could cure her" (Luke 8:43). We can only imagine the ways she was medically examined and treated by these physicians, many of whom we would today call quacks or charlatans. No doubt, each one assured her their cure would work, after she paid them. We can assume bleeding was used, as well as poultices and other ways to stop her bleeding. It does not take much imagination to see how these "cures" could be worse than the original condition.

The blood that has issued from her body for twelve years has made her ritually unclean for twelve years. She cannot participate in communal life, let alone worship in the Temple or a synagogue or around the tables of her friends and family. The cost of this dis-ease is immense and crushing.

The trauma of chronic, unexplained illness is legion in our world today. We think of AIDS patients suffering while the whole world assigned a moral disgust to their pain. Chronic illness and chronic pain separate people from community, and often the only offer the community makes is "Have you tried this?" They have tried, and it hasn't worked.

The woman approaches Jesus in her shame, not meeting him directly but furtively. This is an indication of her deeper soul wound, a belief that she is no longer good or worthy of love. She reaches out her exhausted hand to grasp the hem of his garment. When she touches it in faith, she feels in herself that she is healed. Mark's language is twofold: her bleeding stops, and she realizes it stops. Here we see the nature of Jesus' healing. The wound is healed, the bleeding stops—and the awareness of this is a miracle too. It is the miracle she needs, the realization that this was not just in her head. That she had been seen, without being seen—heard, without being heard. This is what the wounded of the world long for, someone to acknowledge that what is happening inside them is real and credible.

In this moment the woman becomes, to skeptical eyes, fully human, an equal to Jesus, who must be called to account for her bold faith that manifests in this grabbing of cloth. Imagine all the cloths, fragments of old robes, that she used to stanch her bleeding over those twelve years. It is staggering to behold. Then imagine that cloth of Jesus she grabs hold of, never to let go.

Jesus knows what she has been through. He believes her whole story, every bit of it. He includes her in his community. The suffering of twelve years changes in an instant, and a new life opens up before her. She is in fear and trembling as she falls before Jesus, claiming her truth that she was the one who grabbed his clothing.

And so we do this too. Just as her shame drove her to grab only the edge, the fringe of Jesus, so we are sometimes only able to grab the fringe of Jesus. We watch a TV preacher from a distance, we listen to a podcast, we overhear a conversation but don't enter it. We watch, observe, and slowly snake our hand out to grab just the edge. We cannot do more than that in our post-traumatic state. Perhaps professional Christians, like myself, should not be so quick to label as apathy what is really trauma.

American Christians often wander the great empty cathedrals of Europe in wonder—in wonder of the soaring architecture and in wonder why anyone would want to have church in a place like this. American churches, especially as they skew more Protestant, tend to focus on the personal relationship between the preacher and the listener, emphasizing tight-knit community and interpersonal connection. Only the megachurch and the large Catholic mass can be slipped into and out of easily in the USA. But often this is what post-traumatic seekers need. The ability to escape is essential for us whose trauma was inescapable. Perhaps those soaring skeletons of stone offered this to a war-ridden medieval European population in a way our cozy churches in the round do not.

During the pandemic, when people have varied widely in their comfort level for public gatherings, my church community has allowed each person the freedom to choose their seating location devoid of judgment, since we're all staying far apart outdoors. My desire to "pack 'em in" our small space prior to the pandemic was driven by my obsession with great pictures of a crowded church for our Instagram. So now, in the cathedral of the Texas sky, our post-traumatic parishioners have more room, more safety, and more ability to grab the hem of Christ's garment.

13

The Parable of the Traumatized Son

I occasionally visit the street where I lost my beloved cat, Blue. I had been standing at a food truck with him when he bolted, something I'd never seen him do before. I chased him over a six-foot fence and down the street. He turned a corner, and by the time I got there, looking like an out-of-breath cop, he'd given me the slip. I had been out on the lake with him paddleboarding, something we both enjoy, so I was in my post-swim towel wrap while frantically slapping my flip-flops down on the street as I gave my pathetic chase. After searching every yard and under every car, all I could do was call out Blue's name and weep.

I went back to that location several times in the hours and days that followed, putting up posters and searching fruitlessly. At times I saw him out of the corner of my eye, but when I looked directly, he was not there. When I was home I started to put food out for him before the realization hit me: he was gone.

And he was just a cat. Imagine if it were a son. I once met Francene Wheeler, who lost a tiny son in the Sandy Hook School shooting. She said, "People come up to me and say, 'I can't imagine what you're going through.' Well, you can, you just don't want to." We can imagine, even if we don't have kids ourselves. Our imagination works too well at times. Like Bob Dylan said, "When you've lost everything, you find out you can always lose a little more."[1]

The first son born to Adam and Eve was a murderer, exiled by God and condemned to a life of wandering. If Adam and Eve do not weep for his loss, they weep for the son he killed— righteous Abel. Abraham grips the knife to slit his son's throat to obey the divine voice in his head. David wails, "O my son Absalom, my son, my son Absalom! Would I had died instead of you, O Absalom, my son, my son!" (2 Sam. 18:33).

We know what the Son of God said on the cross, but what did his Father say? There are no words, just silence, a dark sky, and thunder. Once the wailing stops, the black curtain of grief is drawn. And so the father in the parable of the prodigal, traumatized son waits. He sits at the end of the road looking up every so often. He sees his son's approach out of the corner of his eye, but when he focuses, nothing is there. He sits in the heat, in the cold, in the rain, in the blazing sun. As he waits a voice whispers to him, "He's not coming back. This is a waste of time." He despairs and heads home, but the next day he is up before sunrise to go to his perch to watch and wait.

As he waits he is changed. The trauma of loss grinds his soul. He thinks of a thousand fixes—send out search parties, send out friends, write a letter—but he knows deep down his son went away by choice and will not come back because of his pathetic pleading. It is only the crush of real life that will bring him back. And so this knowledge grinds at the father's soul. He weeps, he cries out, he is silent. His heart is pummeled with a million blows. He is faint. He is angry. He is grieving.

Meanwhile his son is living his best life in a far country. He spends with abandon and receives the attention he craved in his father's house. And then, when the money runs out, he gets hired as a pig attendant, a shameful profession for someone in Jesus' world.

The son experiences the trauma of hunger. He stares at the swine slop hungrily, debating whether he should abandon self-respect or preserve what little dignity he has left. Humans in dire circumstances have eaten nearly everything we can imagine, even other humans. It is truly the worst possible solution. Rock bottom is a pig sty, wet and foul.

His resolve to return home comes when he reframes his position in his father's house from son to hired hand. He is no longer worthy to be a son. The wound of trauma tells us we are not worthy of love, status, or acceptance. The outside discomfort and pain speak to an inner emptiness. Our only value is as a commodity, a hired hand, a laborer, a contributor. He feels worthless, hopeless, and useless to everyone, especially the father he nearly extorted to buy his freedom in a far country.

Are traumatized people worth anything? I wonder this sometimes when I think of how my PTSD has made my life more difficult. My disability does not help when I value myself by my abilities. So I turn to other abilities, like running, until I am injured, and then I am worthless again. How long can we live in this cycle of grasping a reason to live, then losing it as quick as it came?

And so the son begins the long, lonely, uncertain walk to his father's house. Does he hasten his steps or dawdle, unsure if he should turn back? Step by step he makes it to the edge of his father's fields. And then he sees his father—an old man with his skirts girded up, running toward him. He is running like a twelve-year-old boy, this old man. His beard is flapping in the wind. He is ridiculously happy. He grabs his son and announces, "This son of mine was dead and is alive again; he was lost and is found!" (Luke 15:24).

But the father does not get the same son back. He gets a son who has been through the roller coaster of the world's suffering. He has looked into the abyss and the abyss has looked back into him. He is much older than his years should make him. The son has aged, and so has the father. They are both in a new, post-traumatic world. All they know is that the son was dead and now is alive.

And that is all they need to know. The worth of the son is because he is a son. The love of the father is because he is the father. Nothing else really matters. Traumatized people need to know they are valued simply for being, not for doing. You are enough, the father says with his embrace. And the father cannot stop there. Visible signs of his love are given, the fatted calf is killed, and feasting ensues. He wants his son to know, beyond the shadow of a doubt, that he is valued, loved, accepted.

What is your visible sign of God's love for your post-traumatic life? Is there something you have or have experienced that you can point to, touch, hold? For many Christians, the sacraments, especially Holy Communion, function as a tangible intangible, a physical sign that points to a deeper reality in the spiritual world. Sometimes we need something to hold, touch, eat, when our minds and hearts are racing like a boat propeller pulled out of the water.

The word *sacrament* is from the Latin for "pledge," or sometimes "oath." It was the Roman soldier's oath to follow orders. The word points to the promise and oath of God toward us. When we participate in it, it participates in us. We eat the holy food for holy people, even after we've been through hell. Like the old father in the story, God comes to us running in the sacraments.

I am glad to report that I found my cat. After I searched high and low, someone saw him crawling out of an old church building, about 300 yards from where he took off. While I was searching for him, I imagined what it would be like to find him hiding in a garage. I imagined how happy I would be and how I would hug him and squeeze him.

But when I went to the church and tried to lure him out into the open, he didn't want to come. I grew tense and angry at his hesitancy. Didn't he know I had been looking for him? Didn't he know I had walked every inch of the neighborhood and put up hundreds of flyers at all hours of the day and night in the Texas sun? No, he didn't. To get him to come out from under the building, I lay down on the sidewalk near his hidey-hole. The mosquitoes feasted on me and the fire ants bit me, but I stayed calm until he hesitantly came out of hiding and lay next to me.

He was more traumatized than I was, and I needed to go at his pace, rather than my own. This is what God does for us. God waits for us so that our return to God is our thing, not just his thing. The need for traumatized people or cats to escape is real and is a prerequisite for any reconciliation. Sometimes God lies down among the mosquitos and ants and simply waits for us.

14
Healing the Traumatized Daughter

A number of years ago, when I worked at St. Mark's Episcopal Church in Austin, we hired three actors to dramatically perform the Gospel of Mark on St. Mark's Feast Day. I had heard it takes about an hour to read the whole Gospel out loud, but with a few musical interludes and the sheer drama of the book, it took around two.

My first impression of the event was that it was awesome, that it was breathtaking. This is how the Gospels were meant to be experienced, as a play. In fact, if the Gospels were read as literature and were assigned to a genre, it would be drama.

The second impression I had was there are a lot of demons in Mark's Gospel. Stories with demons in them seemed to happen every couple of minutes in the drama. Despite the ubiquity of demons in the stories of Jesus, Christians today are not of one mind on this subject.

What is a demon? It's a pretty basic question, really, but one you probably shouldn't discuss at work or on a first date. Even as a pastor and writer, I am careful not to say too much for two reasons. I don't want people to think I'm unhinged. I also don't want to invite demonic attention. So I will proceed with caution, trying not to sound too unscientific or to stir up curiosities that will not come to good ends.

My first observation of how demons are described in Jesus' world is that there are several interchangeable terms. "Demon" is used in Matthew in the story of the Syrophoenician woman (15:21–28), whereas "unclean spirit" is used in Mark (7:24–30). These terms seem to be interchangeable, referring to the same entity. Demons are spirits, incorporeal. They do not have bodies but seem to seek bodies—even the bodies of animals, as we see in the story with the legion of demons who enter a herd of swine (Mark 5:1–20).

When this woman meets Jesus, she says, "My daughter is tormented by a demon." The most wooden translation of her Greek would be "My daughter is demonized." Whatever was happening to this girl, it was tormenting enough for her mother to go to great lengths for help. Another story from the Gospels has a demonized boy throwing himself in a fire, to the great panic of his parents. From this I think it is safe to say that the hallmark of demonization is self-destruction.

Demons causing people to be self-destructive is how we talk about it in secular society today. "He had a lot of demons" we say of the Vietnam veteran who drank himself to death. We drink "spirits," and many used to speak of the dangers of "demon rum." There is a force that takes hold of a person when they drink alcohol that often leads down the path of self-destruction. In the book of Acts, the filling by the Holy Spirit at Pentecost is contrasted with being drunk—indicating that the behavior is similar.

The self-destructive behavior coupled with the loss of autonomy must have been a hellish experience for the demonized people in the world of Jesus, as it is for our day as well. If there is a link between demonization and trauma, it is impossible to know in every case. But we must remain open to the connection and listen to how traumatized people talk about their experience with the demonic.

Karl Marlantes writes about this connection in his book *What It Is Like to Go to War*. Marlantes felt an evil presence stalking him after his traumatic experiences in Vietnam. In a special service with a priest, he felt that presence leave for good. Sylvia Fraser, an incest survivor, says it this way:

> I have more convulsions as my body acts out other scenarios, sometimes springing from nightmares, leaving my throat ulcerated and my stomach nauseated. So powerful are these contractions that sometimes I feel as if I were struggling for breath against a slimy lichen clinging to my chest, invoking thoughts of the incubus who, in medieval folklore, raped sleeping women who then gave birth to demons. . . . In a more superstitious society, I might have been diagnosed as a child possessed by the devil. What, in fact, I had been possessed by was daddy's forked instrument—the devil in man.[1]

There is a veil between the psychiatric and the demonic that is not easy to distinguish. Demonized persons are vulnerable, just as mentally ill persons are vulnerable, and there are legions standing ready to do them harm with both good intentions and bad. This is part of the tragedy of trauma, and the aftermath. So many mentally ill persons have been harmed by exorcism-obsessed clergy, and so many have been harmed by psychiatrists who shocked, lobotomized, and experimented on them.

I have long been curious about the sheer volume of demon stories in the Gospels, since they are not a major feature of most other sections of the Bible. Is there a link between the demonic and the oppressive empires of this world that seek to oppress and dominate? Walter Wink thought so. He wrote that there were Jews and Christians in the first century who "perceived in the Roman Empire a demonic spirituality."[2] In their quest for power, the Romans tapped into the evil powers of this world and were empowered to do evil on a grand scale. The people in Jesus' day lived under the burden of Roman occupation. Their presence in the Gospels is ubiquitous. Their presence is assumed on every page, even if not addressed directly. And this situation hurt people, especially the children whose behavior manifested the dis-ease of the society.

In Matthew 15:21–28, it is a little child, a daughter of a
Gentile woman, whom Jesus delivers from a demon. Jesus does
not launch into a lecture about demons as I have done above,
but he refuses to help, on the grounds that he must serve his
own people first before he serves the Gentiles: "It is not fair to
take the children's food and throw it to the dogs."

That he calls her a dog would not be surprising in his world
(even if we are shocked that Jesus could be so dismissive). But
her answer is surprising, in that world and ours: "Yes, Lord,
yet even the dogs eat the crumbs that fall from their masters'
table." She tells him he can do it, he just doesn't want to. This
woman who has experienced the trauma of a demonized child
goes head-to-head with Jesus and wins. She has nothing else to
give. She will leave it all on the track. She has burned all her
bridges, spiked all her guns, salted all her fields. She will not
go home without his agreement to heal her daughter. The hell
of her present is far worse than any rejection he could give her.

I see in this woman the refugees banging on the gate of the
airport, the desperate citizens marching against the regime as the
soldiers cock their rifles, the proud veteran who walks into the VA
clinic because he has finally become suicidal enough to be scared.
The desperation of the traumatized, the post-traumatic rage, is
real, and Jesus feels it in her words and heals the daughter.

An officer in my unit told me about her homecoming after
our deployment to Iraq. She had come back two weeks before
the rest of us to arrange for shipping our vehicles and equip-
ment. She arrived at the army base late and went to the on-base
hotel. Although she had made a reservation, it had been lost.
She told me, "There's two kinds of mad: mad, and Iraq mad. I
got Iraq mad." She got a room. What she described I have felt
too. It's an irrational response to being trapped in a traumatic
situation. It's a survival instinct that kicks in. It is sometimes
the thing that saves us.

And it is this post-traumatic rage that saves the Gentile
woman's daughter. And Jesus says, "Great is your faith." Can
post-traumatic faith be great? Yes—Jesus says so. And deep
down, I hope you know it too.

15

Post-Traumatic Exorcism

We can picture them now, standing in formation on the outskirts of a battlefield, the day after all hell was unleashed there. An order is read aloud, there is silent shuffling in the formation, and the men now gather in their squads, in groups of ten. They draw straws, and in each group of ten there is one who stares at his short straw in horror. Some of these unlucky short-straw men vomit. Some run, only to be grabbed by their squad mates. Some are brave and look each of the nine in the eye, their last vision of the men who will beat them with clubs until they die.

The clubbing is swift and merciless. Blood spatters on the tunics of the men who attack their unlucky squad mate. They are just following orders, the orders of decimation. This is the punishment for a unit that fled before the enemy, a natural reaction for most humans, but a death sentence for a Roman soldier. *Decimation* means "the removal of a tenth" and was used throughout Roman military history to punish the few for the insubordination of the many. The military power of Rome depended on each soldier not running away, even when he knew he would die if he stayed put.

In joining the army, Roman soldiers surrendered their civil rights. They swore obedience to the emperor and to never desert the service. They also swore they would not seek to avoid death. They gave up their inherent right to self-preservation, from fleeing danger, from being human.

Their oaths were tested on the battlefield when the hordes of painted barbarians ran shrieking toward them. Charles Glass's book *The Deserters: A Hidden History of World War II* shows how in this more recent war, the tens of thousands of deserters were willing to gamble a court-martial and firing squad for their own self-perseveration. In other words, most of these men were sure they were going to die in combat because of their incompetent leadership, the strength of the enemy, or their own high-risk job in their unit. Untreated mental health conditions due to the sheer horror of combat also contributed to the desertions in that war. It is not hard to imagine these same factors contributing to desertions and cowardice in all wars, both ancient and modern.

War is scary, and sometimes the flood of fear snaps the thin thread that attaches our civil selves to reality. When the thread snaps, fear floods the body and the body runs for safety. While Christians are familiar with Jesus sweating drops of blood in the Garden of Gethsemane, other attestations of this strange condition are found in Aristotle, who describes animals that sweat blood, and in a story told by Leonardo Da Vinci about a soldier who sweats blood before a battle because he is afraid.[1]

Battlefields are confusing places, and so military discipline seeks to create a buffer, a false reality, around each combatant. If soldiers are more scared of the consequences of fleeing, they will stand. The ways they eat, sleep, walk, and shit maximize the self-discipline needed to stand and face an army in the field. But in the end, soldiers fight for the buddy on their left, the buddy on their right. And they die for the buddy on their left, the buddy on their right.

Soldiers do not do this because they inherently love their squad mates; they do this because one day they wake up to the horror that no one cares about them. The commander doesn't care, the politician doesn't care, and maybe their sweetheart doesn't care either. Their small canvas tent is their universe, their world, their family. In addition to decimation, one of the punishments meted out to cowardly units in the Roman army was sleeping outside the entrenched military camp. Being outside the unit, outside the wire, is a peculiar torture. Soldiers will do anything to get back inside. They will even beat to death their fellow squad mate with the short straw.

Moral injury is an emerging field of study that focuses on the loss of innocence, the loss of one's sense of goodness, experienced by soldiers and other people who often violate their own moral code. Many violate their own moral code by "just following orders." The regret, remorse, contrition happens later, and the symptoms of moral injury can look a lot like PTSD symptoms.

If we get PTSD from being the prey, we get moral injury from being the predator. Human life offers us numerous opportunities to violate our own moral code, to do the thing we thought we'd never do, and military life layers on more morally fraught choices. We can imagine service in the Roman army offering numerous opportunities for moral injury.

Jesus meets a man whom scholar and Iraq war veteran Michael Yandell suggests is a morally injured Roman soldier.[2] Matthew, Mark, and Luke go into great detail about this encounter in the tombs on the other side of the Sea of Galilee.

We meet this man who lives in the tombs, isolated from his community, living a half-life among the dead. He has been placed here, sent here, confined here by his village since he can no longer live among his neighbors. They have tried to restrain him with chains, but he has broken them into pieces with his unnatural strength and intensity. He is scary, a vision of horror, barely recognizable as human.

He lives, if that is an appropriate term, night and day among the dead, howling and cutting himself with rocks. He carries in him the demonic attributes of self-destruction, but he does not die. He is perpetually tormented, tortured, left for dead. If he is a soldier, this is a familiar place. In combat we cross a line of death where we grow familiar and comfortable with our own demise. Soldiers meditate on how it will happen, how it will feel. In a few days, the present reality of dying becomes OK. It is a numbness few recover from. This half-life is preferable to life, but it is strange to behold for the untraumatized. They do not know what it is like to prefer death to the changes and chances of ordinary life.

Cutting is most closely associated with the young; this kind of self-harm starts in most people around age thirteen. Children who have endured severe trauma turn to cutting to achieve a "feeling of calm and relief," Judith Herman writes. "Physical pain is much preferable to the emotional pain that it replaces. As one survivor explains: 'I do it to prove I exist.'"[3]

I am thankful for the healing work therapists and psychiatrists do for people struggling with self-harming behaviors like cutting. If you or someone you know is suffering this way, please notify your doctor, a therapist, or someone else you can trust. This should probably be printed in the header of each page of this book. I'm a patient for my PTSD, my anxiety, and other things that affect my relationships and employment. You should be too if you're reading this book. While we must not be tempted to diagnose biblical characters across the space of 2,000 years and the wisps of long-dried ink, behavior is behavior, and we can only but notice the other people in biblical literature who cut themselves.

When the prophet Elijah calls the hundreds of prophets of Ba'al to Mt. Carmel for a showdown, the prophets of Ba'al plead with their god to consume their sacrifice with fire. They plead with their songs, their cries, and then with their blood. They cut themselves with knives and javelins until their blood gushes out in hopes their silent god will hear them. The demons always demand blood, and these possessed prophets offer theirs in rivers. Indeed, the demonic forces that possess the nations of the earth in their drive for power always get theirs.

The demons get their blood in the trenches of World War I and in the mountain passes of Afghanistan. There the blood of thousands is offered, but the demons' thirst never ends. Even those who survive the demonic orgy of war still know they owe. The demons must get their share, so we cut, and we bleed, and our life goes out of us.

And so this scarred man staggers zombie-like to Jesus crying out in a loud voice, "What have you to do with me, Jesus, Son of the Most High God? I adjure you by God, do not torment me" (Mark 5:7). We cannot know who is speaking; is it the man, the demon, or someone else? The fear is palpable. The man is falling on his knees begging Jesus to leave him alone.

But Jesus cannot leave him alone. When all others have gone away, Jesus stays. In the croaking voice of this raging man can be heard a prayer.

> JESUS: "What is your name?"
>
> MAN: "My name is Legion, for we are many."

A legion was the largest Roman army unit, consisting of around 2,000 soldiers. The heavy infantry soldiers in Roman legions were all Roman citizens, and in Jesus' day they were unstoppable. No one could beat a Roman legion. The power of the legion flowed down from the top to the bottom. Each layer of leadership exacted more from the one below it, and it is the legionnaire who carried the weight on his back. And now this legionnaire who participated in the violence of the legion finds the violence of the legion participating in him. He has become that which he feared. He may have escaped the legion, but the legion has not escaped him. He embodies the legion's trauma.

But Jesus stays with him.

His deliverance from the legion takes place as Jesus sends the demons into the bodies of a herd of swine nearby. As 2,000 pigs stampede headlong off a cliff and into a watery grave, his healing begins. The legion of pigs stampedes away, taking with them his memories of his time in the Roman legion (Mark 5:13).

And we can see him now, sitting calmly with Jesus, "clothed and in his right mind." It is as if he is a completely different person, or as if he is now the person he was always meant to be, before he joined the legion and did the legion's work.

The bar for healing may seem low. Clothed and self-controlled is not an achievement that will get applause, but it is the basic building block of living in community, and this man's healing by Jesus gives him his life back. It is his old life back as well as a completely new life. He is now instructed to tell his story to his community, which must include his chains, the tombs, the scars on his forearms, the legion. It must also include Jesus, for it was through his encounter with Jesus that he found himself once again.

If a legion has left us, we must bear witness to that deliverance, because we are not the only ones who are called Legion, for we are many. There are others out there waiting to hear our story, and that story may be just the thing that brings them to seek help for themselves.

16
The Rich Man and Traumatized Lazarus

The feral dogs lick your sores, and you've lost the energy to shoo them away. How did you get here? We ask this of Lazarus, who sits by the gate of the rich man in Luke 16, and we ask this of all the men and women who lie in our city streets.

What tales they tell when we sit and listen. They tell us of childhoods ruptured by abuse, of parents hitting, uncles raping, mothers abandoning, militaries failing their veterans. Their bodies and minds traumatized, their only comfort is the oversized can of beer they consume at all hours of the day and night. And once they're on the street, literally sleeping on the street, it's hard to move from there. Oh, they move—from bridge to bridge, sidewalk to sidewalk—but they're never anywhere for long. A couple weeks under a bridge feels like a long time, but it's not a long time compared to living in a house. They get nickeled and dimed. With no address, no job, no life, they stay in that orbit like a piece of space junk. It's a declining orbit, but it's slow. Eventually, even if they get off the street, their liver won't last long, especially if they keep hanging on to that big beer can.

There's always a skeptic with stories about homeless men and women who have houses somewhere and drive Mercedes cars to their corner to panhandle, pocketing hundreds a day. What a lie. Each person on the street is visible, although they may feel invisible. Each might look the same to our jaded eye, but they are each gloriously unique.

How thin is the line between Lazarus and the rich man, between Lazarus and me. The rich man has a fence, a wall, a gate between the body of Lazarus and his own body, so that he will not see, smell, and hear his very close neighbor. Without the wall and gate, he fears that Lazarus will violate every boundary, creeping right up to his table, his bed, his bathtub. That is what the rich man thinks at least. Not only will Lazarus scratch his way into the rich man's house, but he will attract others who are similarly slimy. Like rats, they will gather to feed sneakily off the rich man, fouling the water in the pool. Boundaries, gates, walls, jagged glass, benches with arches in the middle, sidewalks with spikes—all keep the human rats away. The distance is so great that neither can really see the other. Neither can know each other, although they are intimately connected.

The rich man thinks the distance he has created from Lazarus makes him safe, but it does not. To be in Lazarus's presence is to experience some of the trauma of being Lazarus. The sores are visible, his stench overpowering, his problems unsolvable. He has been offered work, or at least those who have passed by have said he should get a job. But who will hire him? He can barely lie there, let alone look up at our faces.

And then both are dead. The rich man and Lazarus go to the abode of the dead, Lazarus to Abraham's bosom and the rich man to torment in Hades. There, in that place beyond carbon-based life, they still relate to each other across an infinite distance. A great gulf is fixed between them so that one cannot pass to the other. But the great reversal of death has transformed both of them into who they shall be for eternity. The rich man will be in torment, Lazarus in paradise. In spite of the distance between them they are still in relationship, just as we are always in relationship with those who sleep at our gates. Although their trauma has led them there and us here, we are forever connected.

While the rich man knows his fate, how his indifference toward Lazarus has led him to this place of torment, he is still burdened for his five brothers who live the life he used to live. They have walls and gates between them and Lazarus too. He wants to warn them, to send them a message to be kind to the Lazaruses who live at their gates.

But these five brothers won't believe, Abraham says, even if one comes back from the dead to tell them. The walls these rich men have built to keep Lazarus out have blinded them to the outside world. If they cannot see Lazarus, they will not see the prophets that come to them dressed as Lazarus is dressed, in sores and stench.

For them, it is not trauma that makes it hard to believe, but prosperity and ease. Money, and the things it can buy, insulate us and distract us from the world around us, and even ourselves. Our trust is placed in our growing bank account and not on God. Trauma, the wounds of our lives, open our flesh and our blood leaks out, but through that opening comes Jesus, who has five wounds in his body. He is hard to look at, just as it is hard to look at Lazarus. The post-traumatic Jesus is gathering the Lazaruses of the earth from their sidewalks and placing them at his lavish table. He gets them. He knows them. And he invites us to do the same in his kingdom, on earth as it is in heaven.

17

The Friend at Midnight

One of the most comical parables Jesus tells is sometimes called "the Friend at Midnight." It's simple. A friend shows up at your house late at night unexpectedly. You don't have any food for him, and he's been traveling on foot so he's hungry. So you go to another friend's house at midnight and knock on the door, hoping he'll have some bread for your first friend so you can extend the bare minimum of hospitality to a hungry traveler. The second friend doesn't answer the door but yells, "Go away! I'm in bed, my kids are asleep, and the door is locked!" But you're desperate, so you keep knocking and begging. Finally, the friend gets out of bed and opens the door. Jesus says the second friend doesn't give you the bread because he's your friend, but because he's sick of hearing you yell and bang on the door.

I say this story is comical because it makes me wonder if it happened to Jesus. Was he the friend traveling, the friend in bed, or the friend banging on the door? I also get a little smile on my face when I read this story because it's about grown-ups having friends who annoy each other. Not everything is about trauma, even if this book may sometimes hint at this.

Friends who have stayed with me in my post-traumatic life have been nothing short of life giving. Without them, I cannot imagine being alive now. I have been an annoying friend when I'm spiraling, finding it impossible to feel at ease with anything. I've had friends give me hope when I couldn't see anything at all getting better. Friends show us we are not alone, and this saves lives.

Jesus' story about these friends is about prayer. Sometimes it is our persistence in prayer that opens the locked door. Sometimes it is our annoying entreaties that open the locked door. I've prayed for many people this way as I've seen them spiral by text, on a social media post, or in person. When a friend is hurting, there often seems to be nothing we can do but weep and pray. We can also recommend help such as therapy or even a trip to the ER, but it feels like we have no power to help our friend.

It is the persistent friend who gets the answer, however. It is the friend who doesn't give up but keeps annoying, keeps pestering, keeps knocking on the door. After all, we know the heart of our friend. We know that no matter how tired they are, somewhere in that tired mind and heart there is a spark of love for us to which they will eventually respond.

Jesus taught his disciples to pray this way because he too felt the silence of God in his entreaties and whispered prayers. In his incarnation we know God took on human flesh, but we forget he took on time as well. All our flesh is bound by time. It must have been a sudden lurch for Jesus when he entered time, like when a bus driver hits the brakes and you're walking down the aisle to your seat. The Father's answers to the Son's cries took forever and sometimes never came. In the Garden of Gethsemane, the Father is silent. On the cross, the Father is silent, even as the Son pours his life out, saying, "My God, my God, why have you forsaken me!"

One of the symptoms of PTSD in the American Psychiatric Association's diagnostic manual is "persistent and exaggerated negative beliefs or expectations about oneself, others, or the world."[1] Can this symptom affect the way we pray? I think it can. When we pray, we have to believe, if only a little, that there is a God who hears and can act. Even though our belief is in constant flux, and sometimes we wonder if we have it, that kernel of belief is a positive thing. Faith empowers, uplifts, gives strength. PTSD causes our belief to falter and to not perceive reality accurately. We cannot believe we are worthy of love.

"What father among you, if his son asks for a fish, will instead give him a serpent?" Jesus asks. "Or if he asks for an egg, will give him a scorpion?" (Luke 11:11–12 RSV). Trauma warps our perceptions of the world. Is this because one of the key elements of trauma is betrayal? Trauma, the loss of the illusion of safety, means we think we are seeing clearly but are not. Flashbacks and intrusive memories are proof that we may be reacting to events that are not happening in the reality we share with our fellow humans.

A post-traumatic person might believe she'd get the snake when she asks for a fish. Where was my earthly father when the shit hit the fan? If he could turn his back then, why wouldn't God do it too? Trust is hard to build, and we who have lost our trust take nearly as long as God takes to answer us.

Post-traumatic people need a post-traumatic God. Post-traumatic people need to meet "the God who appears when God disappears in the anxiety of doubt and fear," as trauma-tized theologian Paul Tillich said.[2] I discuss this search for a new God in more depth in my earlier book, *Post-Traumatic God*. The post-traumatic God is the God that Jesus describes as someone who wants to give us good gifts.

In an early stage of one's healing journey, therapy, or treatment for PTSD and trauma, you might not be able to feel that God would give you something good. Perhaps this is why Jesus taught his disciples to pray a prayer that frames all other prayers. The Lord's Prayer, with its brevity and comprehen-siveness, stretches us to consider the basic relationship we have with God, especially for practical matters like forgiveness and our daily food. This prayer and others can slowly create spaces for God's presence to fill inside us. Maybe it's only a glimpse we will see, but a glimpse of a loving father can sustain an orphan for a lifetime.

So practice prayer, out loud, with friends if possible. This is one of the benefits of our Anglican Daily Office practice. The Services of Daily Morning and Evening Prayer frame the day with prayer, and I am always surprised how God speaks to me through these words written so long ago. The psalms have this effect too. It is little wonder so many traumatized soldiers from medieval wars joined monasteries. The repetitive, rhythmic chanting of the psalms that crystallize the wide range of human emotion must have been what sustained many of them. After all, many of the psalms are said to have been written by a person who knew the trauma of war personally—King David.

18

Post-Traumatic Testament

Every so often I'll hear someone refer to a "more Old Testament God," meaning an angry, vindictive deity. Sometimes I hear it from a regular church attender, which is always a shock. I try not to visibly cringe or launch into a lecture, but it's not easy.

That there is a different, meaner god in the Old Testament is not a new observation. The wealthy ship owner, bishop's kid, and heretic Marcion posited this in the early days of Christianity. He even drew up a list of acceptable New Testament books for everyone to read. Incidentally, his list of books is the earliest "canon" of the New Testament of interest to scholars who are doing their darnedest to figure out which books belong in the Bible today. Thankfully, for the purposes of this book, few argue with the inclusion of Matthew, Mark, Luke, and John.

Marcion's basic premise was that the god of the Old Testament is incompatible with the teachings of Jesus, especially about violence. Marcion was correct in his assessment. The violent things God does and says in the Old Testament do seem contradictory to how Christians understand the teachings of Jesus, as long as they understand Jesus' teachings to be all flowers and sunshine.

I work as a pastor, on the retail end of theology and biblical studies, you could say, so my perspective on terminology is
shaped by my interactions with nonprofessionals. There clearly
is a problem of perception if people are still thinking like Marcion in the twenty-first century. The failure is in us, the pastors
and teachers of the land. We have failed to show the love of
God in the Old Testament and the wrath and judgment of
God in the New Testament. We have also failed to read the
Bible through a post-traumatic lens, the lens with which it was
written and through which it was read by its first readers and
most readers throughout biblical and church history.

So much of our discomfort with judgment and wrath is a
mark of our privilege, mine included. Victims of injustice want
justice and write about it. Sometimes their cry for justice seems
to be too much to nontraumatized readers. When the psalmist sings, "O God, break the teeth in their mouths" (Ps. 58:6),
the psalmist is crying out about how the powerful wicked are
making unjust court rulings against the poor and innocent of
the land. This is a cry from below that is always uncomfortable to hear. In our day, white people question the violence
in rap music in similar ways. A community traumatized by
centuries of racial discrimination will produce art that reflects
that trauma. This is a sign of healing in many cases, and the
discomfort of the listener is the goal, an essential ingredient
in a healing process that involves not just the individual traumatized person but the whole community who caused and
received the trauma.

Sometimes love looks like justice, restoration, the removal
of the person or group causing the wounds. And the passion-
ate love of God is on every page of the Old Testament. God
says, "Fear not, for I have redeemed you; I have called you by
name, you are mine. When you pass through the waters, I will
be with you; and through the rivers, they shall not overwhelm
you; when you walk through fire you shall not be burned, and
the flame shall not consume you" (Isa. 43:1b–2 ESV). Love
in the Old Testament is sentimental at times, but mostly it
is highly practical—saving you from danger, bringing justice

to meet injustice, staying with you in hardship and despair. If we cannot see the love of God in the Old Testament, we have failed to read it plainly.

Whenever I hear people complain that "the God of the Old Testament is mean," I lament the failure of our language. The word "testament" is nearly obsolete in modern, nonreligious English, with the exception of "last will and testament." Maybe we should go back to "covenant," since it implies a relationship, for this is precisely what "testament" in "Old Testament" means. We have a record of God's covenant with God's people. "New covenant" is a term that comes from the Old Testament in Jeremiah. The prophecy says God will make a "new covenant" with Israel and Judah. Christians believe that God inaugurated this covenant in Jesus Christ, who himself is the mediator of the covenant. This does not invalidate the old in the same way the second and third movies of a trilogy don't make the first film irrelevant. In fact, the first movie of a trilogy takes on new meaning for those who've seen the second and the third. Like all metaphors, this one is incomplete, but I think it is helpful.

Seeing the love and kindness of God in the Old Testament helps us avoid Marcion's death trap, but it is only when we see the wrath and judgment of God in the New Testament that we can emerge with both testaments in hand.

"Nice Jesus" was probably a product of the Sunday school, itself a byword for overly sentimental and simplistic teaching in many churches. "Sweetness and light Jesus" fades fast when we read about Jesus in the Bible. That Jesus takes his place next to "hippie Jesus" and all the other Jesuses the prosperity gospel preachers, right-wing politicians, and everyone else sees. We all project onto Jesus that which we want to see, and I hope the post-traumatic Jesus will not end up in this company. The danger is there, for sure, so we must continue to return to the texts so that our study of Jesus is grounded in the earliest witnesses to who he was and what he said and did. Each follower of Jesus, each community, has to find the Jesus they need in the moment, but they must guard against assuming that that

Jesus is the Jesus everyone needs in all times and places. It is unlikely I will get invited to any kids' Sunday school classes to speak about the post-traumatic Jesus.

In Mark 9:42, Jesus says, "If any of you put a stumbling block before one of these little ones who believe in me, it would be better for you if a great millstone were hung around your neck and you were thrown into the sea." This statement has always struck me for how violent it is, and how unqualified it is too. Where is forgiveness, mercy, love in this punishment? But it is this Jesus we must listen to in order to truly understand that Jesus is on your side, not your abuser's side. Jesus is upset about what happened to you. Jesus wants to toss your abusers into the sea with a giant stone hung around their neck so they'll gurgle down to the bottom forever. When you're ranting at the heavens about what they did to you, the post-traumatic Jesus doesn't step in and ask you to tone it down a bit. He joins you in your raw anger and grief. He helps you get that giant millstone ready for the toss.

19

Post-Traumatic Adultery

Affairs aren't about romance or sex but about how little we mean to each other. They're also traumatic, especially for the betrayed partner. While the DSM-5 does not include affairs in its description of PTSD, psychologists see an overlap of PTSD symptoms for people who have been betrayed. Some psychologists, most notably Dennis Ortman, see the trauma of an affair to be worth its own four-letter acronym: PISD (post-infidelity stress disorder).[1] If you've been the betrayed party in a marriage, like me many years ago, you know this is not a stretch by any means. Affairs are traumatic because they are a betrayal of trust.

There are numerous affairs in the Gospels. The highest-profile affair is the one Herod Antipas conducts with his brother's wife. John the Baptist's condemnation of this relationship is what causes his beheading. The unnamed woman who is caught in the act of adultery in John 8 is still generating controversy two thousand years later.

The latest dustup about her concerns whether she's even real. Because her story is omitted in some very early manuscripts of the New Testament, many modern translations of

the Bible have notes like this one from the NRSV: "The most
ancient authorities lack 7.53–8.11; other authorities add the
passage here or after 7.36 or after 21.25 or after Luke 21.38,
with variations of text; some mark the passage as doubtful."
St. Augustine quipped that someone cut this story out of the
Gospel out of fear, "lest their wives should be given impunity
in sinning."

And so we meet this cheating woman in John's Gospel,
and the meeting is already uncomfortable—but not nearly so
awkward as if it had been us she cheated on. Would we see
the story differently in that case? We never know how we will
feel until something happens to us. Imagining trauma never
really works.

The men who bring the woman to Jesus insist that she
was caught in the very act of adultery, in flagrante delicto,
in blazing offense. That she was caught alone, in this sexual
offense, is notable to every reader of the story. What is good
for the goose is not good for the gander, and the gander in this
story escapes judgment. The notable absence of the woman's
partner, who would have been with her when she was caught,
may indicate she is being framed. The inequality of how we
treat women vis-à-vis men in sexual offenses is staggering the
world over.

No matter how we see this story, the woman is now a victim
of something worse than adultery—a lynch mob. They want
to stone her, and they want Jesus' approval of this allegedly
lawful punishment. They cite the law after all. There is also
here a trap for Jesus. Does he follow Moses or Caesar, who has
forbidden these kinds of lynch mob killings? All capital crimes
must go through Rome, including the crimes Jesus is convicted
of at his sham trial.

If we read this story through a post-traumatic lens, we must
examine what Jesus does to heal here. The first thing he does
is create space. He begins to write in the dirt. No one knows
what he writes. Is it the name of her missing partner in crime?
Is it the names of all the adulterers in the town? Is it a prov-
erb or Bible verse? We might think of God's finger carving his

commandments on the stone tablets for Moses, one of them being the seventh, "Thou shalt not commit adultery." Whatever he writes intrigues the mob, and they seem to calm down a bit in their lust for righteous violence. This mob cannot compete with a man doodling in the dust. Victims of mob violence need immediate protection, and Jesus gives that to her in the only way he can.

This should be our first consideration when anyone comes to us with a marriage problem. The canon law of the Episcopal Church states that the first consideration for priests who learn of a marriage difficulty is the safety of all parties. Each person, their kids, everyone else, must first establish safety. I hope all other church leaders do the same. How many women have been beaten and killed because no one believed them?

"Let anyone among you who is without sin be the first to throw a stone at her," Jesus says. Then Jesus stoops back down and starts writing again. What does he write this time?

When Jesus writes the second time, he has control of the mob. Now he controls where they cast their hate-filled gaze. Victims advocates know how hard it is for victims to testify with their abuser staring at them in the courtroom. One glance can send them into spirals and paralysis, and even silence.

And then the mob disperses, from the oldest to the youngest. This tells me there is some kind of wisdom in the writing on the ground that is first understood by the elders, then the younger men.

We are so quick to associate youth with open-mindedness, the cardinal virtue in a liberal society, but that is not always so. The rise of the alt-right in the 2010s was largely a young person's movement. When we look back on our whole lifetime, marking the places where people showed us grace, mercy, and love, that ought to demand we act the same way. Even if we have received harsh treatment, that should prod us to do the opposite when faced with people who have broken the law and have had the law break them. Grace is always breaking into karma and law. The sacred is always breaking into the profane.

And here, with Jesus and this woman, we see it. We see love that is shown by justice. The mob disperses and they are alone.

> JESUS: "Woman, where are they? Has no one con-
> demned you?" Jesus asks.

> WOMAN: "No one, sir."

> JESUS: "Neither do I condemn you. Go your way, and
> from now on do not sin again." (John 8:10–11)

You can see why St. Augustine claimed that jealous husbands wanted this particular verse gone. Is there no condemnation for adultery? Should there be? The answer lies in our need
for retribution and revenge. When we are faced with mercy
and love, we mistake it for all of society unraveling.

And maybe it has. Maybe the post-traumatic Jesus has come
to do just this, to unravel the cycle of retribution, even in situations where we think it is deserved.

20

The Donkey King

The final week of Jesus' life is a fractured narrative, split up into bite-size chunks by the self-preserving post-traumatic memory so that the trauma of all that happened does not overwhelm the heart and soul of the disciple-narrators who witnessed it. How could they forget how the week started? As on 9/11, the sky was a beautiful blue. There weren't even any clouds. The air was crisp, perfect. It was so peaceful. All traumatic stories begin this way. They are told with a baseline of peace, even if that is a lie. The illusion of safety is only an illusion. It all ends in seconds, in fire and ash.

Jesus' slow ride into the city is at the pace of his grief for his city, his people. There are exuberant shouts, but this feels hollow as he weeps. The juxtaposition between the crowd's cheers and his tears is the great gulf between those who are experiencing trauma and those who ignore it. Jesus is embodying the trauma of the whole world—past, present, and future—and so he weeps. Through his tears he prophesies the city being surrounded by enemies, being crushed to the ground, children dying, stones strewn across the ground. This is the pre-apocalyptic vision of this weeping prophet. He can see it, and like Cassandra who is cursed to see the future, no one will believe him.

"A fire broke out backstage in a theatre," writes Kierke-gaard. "The clown came out to warn the public; they thought it was a joke and applauded. He repeated it; the acclaim was even greater. I think that's just how the world will come to an end: to general applause from wits who believe it's a joke."[1]

Jesus' weeping over Jerusalem's impending destruction is repeated again and again in the Gospels. It is not a detached, dispassionate prediction, but a gut-wrenching, ugly crying gush of raw emotion and grief for what will soon be lost and destroyed. Sometimes all we can do is weep.

It is easy to be cynical about Jesus' prophecies of Jerusalem's destruction as we sit in the comfortable chair of hindsight. We know the city will be destroyed in AD 70. We know this because we have a voluminous contemporary source, Josephus, who wrote *The Jewish War* from his comfortable retirement, telling the story of the city's demise in minute detail. He was there to see it fall, after all.

Josephus, who was from a good family in Jerusalem, was sent to defend Galilee from Roman aggression after the Great Revolt, when the Jews resisted the Romans as they sought to extort more taxes. This was in the reign of Nero, who was not known for his moderation. Since the Jews destroyed an entire Roman legion of 6,000, the might of Rome fell hard. Although most Jews did not want a revolt or the subsequent Roman reprisals, soon the whole land was swept into outright war. Josephus strengthened the defenses of several Galilean cities for the oncoming Roman onslaught but was besieged and surrendered to Rome.

His surrender to Rome tells us something of who he was. Josephus holed up with forty freedom fighters in a dry cave. Underground and in the dark, the fighters told the Romans above they were never coming out. They would kill themselves before becoming Roman slaves or crucifixes. But Josephus had a plan. He rallied the men to each kill the other by standing in a circle and counting down a certain number. Josephus calculated where he should stand in this deadly number game so that he and one other remained. Josephus convinced the last man to surrender with him to the Romans.

Upon surfacing from the cave, Josephus prophesied about the Roman general Vespasian, who had just captured him—that Vespasian would be the next emperor of Rome. From this moment, Josephus, traitor to Jerusalem, accompanied Vespasian and his son Titus to the bitter end of the campaign, when Jerusalem was laid waste.

Who can trust this false prophet of Roman loyalties? This turncoat's account is our main source of information on what happened to the city Jesus wept over. The trauma of the revolt creeps into every page of Josephus's *Jewish War*, and not only in the scenes of violence and destruction but in Josephus's obsession with his rival and nemesis, John of Gishala. Josephus hated him with a passion and described his every move, continuing the revolt that resulted in the destruction of the Temple, the last stand of the rebels.

All this destruction is seen by Jesus with his prophetic eye. We might be tempted to say the authors of the Gospels—writing after the time of Jerusalem's destruction—read these prophecies backward, putting these words in Jesus' mouth to make him look more supernatural or prophetic. While this is certainly a possibility, when we look through the post-traumatic lens, we need not take that cynical option. Jesus feels deeply the impending doom of this city that has long killed the prophets and has been destroyed before. He loves it dearly and knows how the world works. He knows the illusion of safety the crowd is feeling is fleeting, false, and ultimately misleading. He weeps because that is all we can do when we see the world through the lens of trauma.

Those who see the world with post-traumatic eyes can sound like prophets and are often ignored. When the drumbeats of the Iraq invasion began to sound, many Vietnam veterans denounced it, but no one listened. They knew the cost of war and the folly of thinking it would make our lives better. The

post-traumatic writer and Vietnam war veteran Tim O'Brien
says this:

> A true war story is never moral. It does not instruct, nor
> encourage virtue, nor suggest models of proper human
> behavior, nor restrain men from doing the things they have
> always done. If a story seems moral, do not believe it. If
> at the end of a war story you feel uplifted, or if you feel
> that some small bit of rectitude has been salvaged from the
> larger waste, then you have been made the victim of a very
> old and terrible lie. There is no rectitude whatsoever. There
> is no virtue. As a first rule of thumb, therefore, you can tell
> a true war story by its absolute and uncompromising alle-
> giance to obscenity and evil.[2]

And this is an act of love. Jesus says he longs to gather his
people under his wings like a mother hen gathers her chicks.
The post-traumatic love of Jesus is fierce, and bold, and breathtaking. Every step of his final week is a step toward love, and
we must not miss this. His intentionality is seen in every move,
every parable, every touch, every cry of pain. This is the love
that we remember in our suffering and in our war stories, and
it is the love we see when we look into the abyss of human
experience. He has been there, and he is here with us.

So we look up at the thundering sky in terror and see his
giant wings enfolding us.

21
Hypervigilance

The parables and sermons of Jesus' final week have a theme: stay awake. In the Garden of Gethsemane he says this to his disciples while he prays, but he has said this to them before.

His parable of a man going on a journey in Matthew 24:45–51 and 25:14–30 (cf. Mark 14:32–42 and Luke 19:11–26) ends with "Keep awake!" His eerie sentence, "For as the days of Noah were, so will be the coming of the Son of Man" (Matt. 24:37), describes people going about their lives in homes and fields when suddenly one is taken. "Keep awake," he says.

The owner of the house must keep awake so he can stop the thief. The faithful slave stays awake for when the master comes back. He does not get drunk but stays alert for the creaking of the gate and the sound of a horse's hoofbeats. The ten bridesmaids lose half their company because five were not alert enough, not awake enough.

Psychiatrist Elaine Hilberman describes the experience of women traumatized by sexual assault:

Events even remotely connected with violence—sirens, thunder, a door slamming—elicited intense fear. There was chronic apprehension of imminent doom, of something terrible always about to happen. Any symbolic or actual sign of potential danger resulted in increased activity, agitation, pacing, screaming and crying. The women remained vigilant, unable to relax or to sleep. Nightmares were universal, with undisguised themes of violence and danger.[1]

Hypervigilance allows no rest, no relaxation, and no peace. When I came home from Iraq, I was never tired. In spite of an intense running schedule and demanding Army work, I was never drowsy in meetings for about two to three years. I couldn't rest, relax, watch movies, or read books. I had to be on the move, like a shark, always swimming. It was my brain trying to protect me, but it made it impossible for me to sit still, which had grave consequences for relating to other people.

What Jesus is instructing his disciples to do is not hypervigilance, but plain old-fashioned vigilance. Their complacency is what will make them unready when he returns, and they will miss out on that reunion.

Hypervigilance as a symptom of PTSD is debilitating, but nonvigilance can be deadly. Soldiers in war who stop wearing their helmet because of the heat or the weight of it find this out when the rounds start coming down range. The symptom of PTSD I see Jesus addressing for his post-traumatic church is the numbing that happens during or after traumatic events.

In Iraq, I once saw a soldier lying out on the front "hood" of his M1A1 tank with his flak vest wide open to the breeze and his helmet off. This might be seen as bravado—after all, the film *Full Metal Jacket* says the Marines are "the phony tough and the crazy brave." Once someone crosses the line of death, that certain knowledge about how one will surely die, then life can be lived carelessly again.

These two extremes, numbness and hypervigilance, pull on the traumatized mind in both directions, and sometimes the cable snaps. Reality as we perceive it is gone, and a host of fears and anxieties take over like waves of screaming troops. And Jesus knows this about us. He knows we can't always control these responses and symptoms. This is why he commands that our vigilance be proportionate to the event we are waiting for.

He also knows that the event we should be vigilant for is a good event. The clouds of post-traumatic gloom often enshroud our vision of good things ahead. In order to experience good things in our future, we must expect good things in our future. We must wait for them as we wait for the terrible things. We must believe in the power of Jesus' love as much as we believe in the power of evil's destruction.

At its very basic level, for post-traumatic people, faith is believing something good might happen.

22

Post-Traumatic Judas

What can we say of Judas, a man, a human being, who looms so large in the conscience of the Christian world and perhaps beyond it? He is reviled again and again, and yet he remains a mystery.

Is he trying to jumpstart an insurrection against Rome by creating a showdown in court with Jesus? Is he consumed by greed and just wants the quick buck? Does he want Jesus' kingdom of love to fail, so the world can continue to extort and exploit? There are limitless possibilities, all of them subject to the subjective experiences of the commentator. Like Judas himself, I am not immune from temptation.

Through a post-traumatic lens, we must see Judas with compassion, knowing that he is very much like us, full of all the complexities that living on a knife-edge brings. Roman occupation, the hardships of life on the road, and being responsible to feed Jesus' band of followers take their toll. But we must still ask the question: Why betrayal? Everyone breaks, Peter breaks, the other disciples flee in terror, but Judas's work is premeditated, deliberate, and his acknowledgment at his end confirms this.

Whenever there is a mass shooting, we are quick to look for a cause that makes sense to us. If the shooter is a veteran, the shooting makes sense to us. If the shooter is mentally ill, then it makes sense to us. In spite of the fact that most veterans and most mentally ill people don't hurt anyone, and are more likely to hurt themselves, this clarifies things for us. The mind craves meaning, and it will make a meaning in the vacuum of tragedy.

Judas is not ill. If he were, Jesus would have healed him. Judas is evil, and that is much harder to understand in our world, where evil is psychologized and pathologized. People are not evil today; they are toxic. We cut them out of our lives, curate our relationships, cull the herd for the best relational livestock.

Judas is one of the Twelve, a trusted companion of Jesus. The Gospels tell us that Jesus knows what Judas is up to, but Jesus seems to be the only one who can see this. For the Twelve, all is well with Judas—until it isn't.

Michael Card's song about Judas, "Traitor's Look," includes this line: "Only a friend can betray a friend."[1] The betrayal depends on the friendship; otherwise Judas is just another of Jesus' enemies who wants him gone. No, Judas is close, intimate, trusted. He is the last one you'd suspect.

The trauma of betrayal cuts to the bone, and so much trauma is simply betrayal. When mortar rounds hit a chow hall in Baghdad, killing dozens of U.S. soldiers, the survivors kept repeating, "It happened in the chow hall," which is a place where they were supposed to be safe. Sexual trauma is often perpetrated by a close friend, a family member, a date.

Judas is evil because he betrays Jesus to Jesus' enemies. He arranges an event in which Jesus will be arrested, and no one will be able to stop it. Once Jesus is in the physical custody of his enemies, anything can happen to him and few will intervene. This is the focus of the Gospels, not why Judas does what he does. Being in police custody is dangerous in all times and places.

Matthew tells us that Judas repents, returns the money, and hangs himself. His final words hang in the air: "I have sinned by betraying innocent blood" (Matt. 27:4). His moral injury is palpable. He cannot live with himself anymore. His act of grand self-destruction does not exonerate him, but it does make us stare into the abyss of the human condition. Judas' actions of betrayal shout at him and tell him he no longer deserves to live. The Gospels tell us that Satan enters Judas during the Last Supper, but after he betrays Jesus. Therefore, Judas's betrayal is not Satan's doing, but his own. The hanging, however, is the hallmark of Satan. Self-destruction is the goal of the demonic and satanic, and Judas ties the knot and falls to his ignoble end.

Unlike Jesus, there is no trial for Judas. His suicide is the final word. We do not get to sift his motives or cross-examine him. His noose stands in contrast to Jesus' cross, a symbol that takes us into holiness. Judas's noose is the end. "It would have been better for that one not to have been born," Jesus says (Matt. 26:24).

Through my post-traumatic lens, Judas shows us the limits of a post-traumatic memory. If we delve too deeply into the motives, causes, and internal world of our betrayers, we join Judas in his noose, forever choked and subject to wherever the wind spins our gaze round and round, our eyes blank. No, Christians look to the cross for the meaning of suffering and shame, trauma and grace. It is Jesus' death we contemplate, not Judas's.

There is one last story about Judas, although it's not in the Bible but in Christian tradition. What Jesus does on Holy Saturday, the day between the crucifixion on Friday and the resurrection on Sunday, is a mystery. The Apostles' Creed says Jesus descended into hell, presumably on that first Holy Saturday. When he goes there, I imagine that the first person he looks for is his friend Judas. And so Judas is that one lost sheep in the parable. There is no place we can go where Jesus will not go to find us, even hell itself.

23
The Lasting Supper

If the crucifixion is the central traumatic incident of the Gospels, then the Last Supper is the calm before the storm, the one last moment before everything comes undone. It is no wonder it is recounted in detail by each evangelist. They linger over the little moments—as only a post-traumatic narrator can do. "It was perfect, calm," she says, and we know what comes next.

In all the Gospels, we read the Last Supper through the lens of the imminent crucifixion. Every look, every touch, every word is delivered in the shadow of the cross. Jesus' warmth is felt here intensely, the last lingering bit of his love before his body is torn apart by the Romans.

The crucifixion ruins the Last Supper as much as it informs it. Imagine the first time his disciples celebrated Communion, or what became Communion, with each other after his ascension. Did Peter's hand tremble as Jesus held the bread and said, "This is my body"? Do our hands tremble when we hold this bread? The beaten, broken body of Jesus is inseparable from the broken bread at the table, and that fact has formed a hard shell that no amount of modernity can break. We all know, *nearly ,*

deep in our souls, that we are in the presence of trauma when we come to this holy meal, no matter where we find it.

In all the churches I've attended—Baptist, Pentecostal, Episcopal, Catholic, Orthodox—I have felt the weight of this trauma. That this is a commemoration of trauma means my trauma is part of the meal too. No part of my experience, no matter how bitter, is forbidden at this table.

It saddens me that in our quest for reverence, we have often settled for fussy formality at this holy table. But who can dictate the mood of this meal? I certainly cannot. That first Last Supper was so strange, with all its subterfuge, speechifying, and ignorance. "Is it I, Lord?" the disciples say, most of them knowing they would do nothing wrong. But it is. It is I, Lord. We are there at that table with the Twelve and with all the phony-tough disciples who have gathered for the last 2,000 years. We are there in all our splendor and bravado, oblivious to what is about to happen.

I shared this meal in Baghdad during the war there, and the palpable sense of impending doom changed the way the bread and wine tasted. Will I ever taste this meal the same way again? No, I will not, and you will not either. The deeper you explore your trauma, the deeper you will explore this meal and the trauma that flavors it.

For many who have suffered childhood trauma, mealtimes are fraught with anxiety and fear. Judith Herman writes of "terrified silences, forced feeding followed by vomiting, or violent tantrums and throwing of food. Unable to regulate basic biological functions in a safe, consistent, and comforting manner, many survivors develop chronic sleep disturbances, eating disorders, gastrointestinal complaints, and numerous other bodily distress symptoms."[1] Unlike the vision of the heavenly banquet Jesus invites his disciples into, the meals of post-traumatic people seem to do more harm than good.

Perhaps Jesus is not only giving his followers a new way to live, but a new way to eat. By centering the meal on his trauma, our trauma is welcome, taken, broken, eaten, and digested, along with his trauma. The Communion meal works backward

through time. Each time it is observed, we are eating that first
Last Supper with Jesus and his friends. Could the same happen
to our fear-filled memories of spilled milk and monstrous consequences? Could Jesus appear as a guest at those tables of fear?

"You prepare a table before me in the presence of my enemies," Psalm 23:5 comforts us. How is this possible? Most of
us aren't able to eat before a job interview, let alone with someone who wants to do us harm. The presence of the Good Shepherd changes our gut instinct, our hesitancy, even our nausea.
At least the possibility exists that it can. Like everything in this
book, my words are not a substitute for therapy, and no one
should put themselves in harm's way. But we must eat to live,
and if we are to eat, we should eat with Jesus, the Good Shepherd, who shares his traumatic meal with us. At the least we
should say grace over our psychiatric medication, asking God
to bless it for our use and us to thy service.

We are what we eat, after all. And this is the macabre mystery
of this meal and how it has been contemplated ever since that
night. "How can this man give us his flesh to eat?" Jesus' listeners said to him in John 6. It's gross, inappropriate, obscene. It
violates norms, transgresses taboos, and brings up cannibalistic
horror in our minds. And yet this is the antidote to our fears.
This is the comfort food of his body and blood given for us.
We eat in faith so that our trauma might be fused with his and
then transformed into what is now our new life in Christ.

This is as much a miracle as when Jesus fed the 5,000 and
when he rose from the dead. It should not surprise us when he
feeds us this way in this meal. The possibility is there, just as it
was there on that first Last Supper. We are invited to experience this meal again and again until the day we eat it in the
kingdom with Jesus.

24

Sword in the Night

Physical violence causes trauma, literally, "wounds," both in the psychological and physical realm. When Jesus is arrested, there is an outburst of physical violence from Peter, who hacks off the ear of the high priest's servant Malchus. Malchus is named in John's Gospel (18:10) but not any of the others. His name comes from the Hebrew word for "king," and yet he is an enslaved person.

In the dark shuffle of Jesus' arrest in the Garden of Gethsemane, Peter pulls out the sword he is carrying concealed in his tunic. Peter apparently is a terrible swordsman, and his blow glances off the side of Malchus's head, severing his right ear. Assuming Peter is right-handed, the physics of this strike leave us with many questions. Perhaps as if he were using a tennis backhand, Peter has swung with all his might and hit Malchus in the right ear. If his strike was more like an overhand serve, he has sliced the ear from the top down. In the confusion of the moment, the precise details escape all four evangelists.

While Jesus said to turn the other cheek if someone strikes you, he never covered whether you should defend someone else from attack. But Peter's strike is immediately rebuked by the one he was trying to protect. "Put your sword back into its sheath," Jesus says in John's Gospel. "Am I not to drink the cup that the Father has given me?" (John 18:11). In Matthew Jesus says, "For all who take the sword will perish by the sword" (Matt. 26:52). Jesus tells Peter that he has done the opposite of what Jesus wanted him to do.

But Malchus does not strike back. Jesus heals him before anyone strikes back. It seems those who are arresting Jesus are not so concerned about what has happened to Malchus. Either Jesus has healed him before most of those in the dark mob have noticed, or Malchus is expendable. But Malchus is a prestigious person because of his connection to the high priest, so this cannot be the case. Whatever is happening with Malchus, this takes the wind out of Peter's sails. He has failed to protect his teacher and friend. He has failed the Messiah.

For most Americans of a certain economic class, pacifism is a luxury, an indication of privilege. We might call it "spectator pacifism," as it deals with abstractions and ideals from a safe distance. But even pacifists often depend on the violence of others. With overfunded police departments, doorbell cameras, and apps that report even the most banal happenings, violence is someone else's job. We read of it, hear of it, but it stays mostly out of our direct line of sight. Every so often the real violence of the world crashes into ours, and we call it surreal. The trauma of 9/11 did this, the hallmark definition of terrorism.

The right to self-defense is the most basic of human rights, but Jesus said to turn the other cheek if someone strikes you. To surrender such a right voluntarily is remarkable, maybe even supernatural. Defending other people with force is seen as a good thing by nonpacifist Christians, because it is a way of loving your neighbor as yourself.

But here in this garden, in the dark, Jesus offers a new way of living for those who fight to survive. "Put away your sword" is a command to Peter and to us. Many who have had to fight to survive have put up their swords and followed the one who gives us a new way to live and die. He who lives by the sword dies by the sword and, for the most part, never really lives.

St. Martin of Tours, St. Francis of Assisi, and many others served as soldiers before laying down their weapons and living a life of peace and simplicity. This is the path that Jesus offers. How many traumatized people have clung to weapons to secure themselves against that feeling of powerlessness? I didn't carry a weapon in Iraq since I was a chaplain, but I did when I got home. I got rid of that pistol, though, when I found my five-year-old son holding the locked gun case from my closet in his little hands. He was shaking the box. The weapon was unloaded, but that was all I needed to decide never to own another firearm. Here in Texas not a week goes by when a child isn't accidentally killed by a firearm "safely" stored in their home. There are some things worse than my own death.

Because of my PTSD and suicidal thoughts in the past, I don't want to risk becoming a part of the group of veterans who shoot themselves. This method has a 90 percent lethal rate; other methods are only lethal 4 percent of the time. This grim calculation is how I see it, since I have stared into that tunnel of suicide several times in my life. The tunnel is narrow and dark, and no other light gets in. I've escorted numerous people to emergency rooms to be treated for suicidal ideation and attempts, and I'm always surprised by the staff who chide the patient with, "You have two kids! What were you thinking?" That's how dark the tunnel of suicide is. Even kids can't shine a light in there.

"Put away your sword" is a saying of Jesus repeated by his apostle Paul to a suicidal soldier in Philippi (Acts 16:23–40). Sometimes the commands of Christ are very practical and concrete. Put away your sword. Don't hurt your body. Put away the false securities of your post-traumatic world. No weapon will keep us safe from the changes and chances of this life. Only Jesus can do that, and following him will lead us to people and communities that show us a new way to live.

25

Post-Traumatic Cold

In February 2021, during the COVID-19 pandemic, I experienced my first traumatizing natural disaster, the Texas Freeze. While other parts of the country and world regularly drop down into the single digits, this is exceptionally rare in Texas, and our infrastructure was woefully inadequate. The power grid failed early, and since nearly all our heating is tied to electricity, our homes slowly dropped in temperature every hour. Then the water pipes failed, and we supplemented our bottled water by boiling potentially contaminated water on the only working gas stove.

I took in an elderly parishioner who was getting colder and colder in her apartment. We bundled up in a dark, cold house, keeping our children close. For people living in hot climates, severe cold events are rare but traumatic, in that they often involve a breakdown of multiple levels of safety. As the following autumn approached, bringing fall temperatures to Texas, my anxiety started to go up, my body preparing itself for the next big cold disaster. We will be better prepared this time, but we weren't the first time, and that is where my fear still returns to. The body keeps the score and does not care if the traumatic event happens again or not.

We know little about the weather in Jesus' world and life. We know of the storms on the sea that nearly killed him and his disciples. We know of the storm at his crucifixion, but not much else. The only cold weather mentioned in the Gospels is on the night in which he is betrayed. After his arrest in Gethsemane, Jesus is taken to a secretive trial at the house of the high priest. Peter follows at a safe distance in the dark, blending into the shadows of the courtyard. John writes, "Now the slaves and the police had made a charcoal fire because it was cold, and they were standing around it and warming themselves. Peter also was standing with them and warming himself" (John 18:18). How cold? It does not say.

But Peter is cold, so he draws near to the fire, even though it's risky. It is here he is peppered with questions about his relationship to Jesus. With every question he denies knowing Jesus. In a rare literary move for ancient writers, John flashes the camera on Peter at the charcoal fire, then back to Jesus' trial inside the house, then back to Peter again.

We who can turn up the thermostats or even climb into our cars for heat after the football game may not be able to imagine the terror of what it is like to be poorly clothed and exposed to a winter night. The world of Jesus was lit only by fire. Fire made the difference between life and death when the cold snaps came. Jesus tells a story about a family sleeping in a bed all together, presumably for warmth and safety. But Peter is alone in this crowd around the charcoal fire. His answers are as cold as the chilly air. "No, I am not his disciple."

Physical desperation leads to emotional desperation, and Peter is desperate. His need for warmth from the charcoal fire parallels his need for safety from being crucified with Jesus, an act of devotion he promised Jesus he would do for him. He is exposed to the cold, and nearly exposed as a follower of Jesus.

For me, the Texas Freeze was an in-your-face reminder that climate change is real and will affect me and my family directly. Severe fluctuations and extreme weather are the hallmark

patterns of this climate apocalypse. Our desire to protect ourselves from the bitter cold and scorching days has us burning
the fossil fuels whose exhaust poisons our world. Our need to
move fast across the land and sky poisons the air. We have
done these things in our desperation to achieve, to expand, to
consume—but now we are the ones consumed.

We can hope and pray that humans will cooperate to bring
about healing to this planet, but climate trauma will likely
make things more difficult as people have less capacity to think
hopefully. Many will, like Peter, scramble to protect themselves at the expense of everyone else. I hope the church of
Jesus Christ will rise up as one to show a new path forward of
self-denial and reduced consumption. Jesus said that our lives
do not consist of the things we possess. We need warmth, heat,
air-conditioning, and transport, but perhaps not in the quanti-
ties we have them now.

After denying Jesus a total of three times around that charcoal fire, Peter speaks next with Jesus in John 21, on the shore
of the Sea of Galilee where Peter has been fishing. He has gone
back to his old life, the life he knew before Jesus. There is famil-
iarity, if not meaning, in fishing. But when Jesus meets him on
the shore, there is a charcoal fire. The same Greek word is used
here as was used in the scene in the high priest's courtyard in
chapter 18. It is as if Jesus is taking Peter back to the scene of
the crime in some kind of primitive exposure therapy. Did the
charcoal fire trigger Peter, reminding him of his weakness that
drove him to that fire where he denied his messiah?

A fire is convenient for difficult conversations, and difficult
conversations are necessary for good relationships, especially after
trauma. You can look at the burning coals dance in the shadows
instead of the eyes of your friend who left you in the cold. Jesus
gathers his disciples around the charcoal fire. He takes bread and
gives it to them. He does the same with the fish, an obvious
thing to do since they just had a miraculous, abundant catch.
But the bread is pointing to something else. It is the bread of fellowship, the bread of the covenant. Peter receives a tangible sign
of restoration before any verbal or legal reconciliation with Jesus.

After breakfast, Jesus questions Peter three times: "Simon son of John, do you love me more than these?" These three questions are the post-traumatic mirror image of the questions Peter answered in his denial of Jesus: "You are not also one of this man's disciples, are you?" Peter's answer to that question was no, but now he answers, "Yes, Lord, you know that I love you."

When we have a traumatic failure of nerve, just as Peter did, our first hope is that no one will notice. We hope the one we let down will forget and move on. But we know they cannot. Jesus does not forget what Peter did to him. Jesus heals what Peter did to him. Jesus is active in his reconciling work. He meets Peter with an object lesson, a visible symbol of his denial—the charcoal fire. His threefold restoration addresses each denial perfectly, and so when Jesus says, "Feed my sheep," Peter has a new start.

In the life of Jesus, healing seems mostly to be about the timing. And only Jesus knows the timing. Peter's restoration, his healing, happens after what must have seemed like an eternity for Peter. Several weeks go by when Jesus appears and talks, but Peter and Jesus never have "the conversation." For traumatized people, healing, however we define that, takes forever. Herman defines the stages of healing as "establishing safety, reconstructing the trauma story, and restoring the connection between survivors and their community."[1] Stages, steps, phases, journey all describe a linear process that stretches out for quite some time. There are no get-healthy-fast schemes, and anyone who peddles such schemes often inflicts more damage than help.

When Jesus meets Peter at the charcoal fire, Peter is healing from his traumatic experiences too. It is the post-traumatic Jesus that offers trust, a new story, and a new community to Peter. Rather than asking Peter to focus on Jesus, Jesus asks him to feed his sheep, his community of followers. Giving Peter this responsibility indicates Jesus trusts him. Can Jesus trust Peter after what he did to him? Jesus thinks so. Jesus thinks so about you and me too.

26

Post-Traumatic Trial

A judicial system is a substitute for impulsive, personal, and vigilante violence. Gone are the days of family avengers killing those who did their family member wrong. It is the state that prosecutes crimes, not the victim or the victim's family. Instead of raw retribution, we argue. Instead of revenge, we call to the witness stand. It is better this way. Retributive violence gets subdued, made inefficient. Every so often a story will hit the news of an aggrieved father shooting the man who molested his daughter. Deep down we approve, and many will say so publicly. But mostly, we lawyer up and deny everything.

Jesus' trial was traumatic, not in a blood-and-gore way, but in the slow-drip, death-by-a-thousand-cuts way. It holds all the tension of his impending execution in it, but it is all statements, witnesses, arguments. The petty and false arguments about what words he spoke escalate throughout the night, into his brutal beating and humiliation, into his being paraded in front of the mob, and at his bloody cross. And this is the same template for all judicial proceedings, even if they do not end in an execution.

Did he not say himself, "Come to terms quickly with your accuser while you are on the way to court with him, or your accuser may hand you over to the judge, and the judge to the guard, and you will be thrown into prison" (Matt. 5:25)? What we think of as justice escalates quickly into the cutting of flesh and the breaking of bone.

Even our efforts to seek justice for victims of violent trauma can be in itself traumatic. "If one set out by design to devise a system for provoking intrusive post-traumatic symptoms, one could not do better than a court of law," writes Herman. It is not uncommon for women to describe their justice proceedings as "being raped a second time."[1] Even in the "best" circumstances of justice, the original trauma participates in the justice, and many victims choose to try to just "let it go" rather than rehash and reexperience the events that turned their world upside down. When Jesus goes to trial, he is with us in our traumatizing quest for justice.

But there is no justice on this night. There is rarely justice in the dark of night, only revenge. The whole world has gathered to condemn this man, the leaders of the faith and the representatives of the empire. It is a wonder they bother to have a trial at all. Here we glimpse the banality of evil, the speech of the serial killer before he maims, the Nazi formation before the gas chamber, the pomp and circumstance of sheer and utter cruelty. We often think of the chaos of trauma, but here it appears orderly and just, venerable and disciplined. It is, however, simply rage spread thin, the manifestation of the stomach ulcers of those who want Jesus dead and gone. They will crucify him, even if they must do it with their own hands.

Jesus' life is bookended by courtroom drama. In the beginning we see Herod in his courtroom, for that is what a throne room is, ordering baby Jesus' execution. At the end, it is a crowded high priest's house, Herod's son's palace, and Pilate's military court that gives him a second death sentence. This was a shadow he lived in his whole life and spoke of often.

Like trauma survivors the world over, did Jesus experience these threats creeping in uninvited when he laughed with his friends? Did they shadow his sunny days and haunt his dark nights? We know he often went to be alone, to express to God the inexpressible—alone, in the dark, praying his high priestly prayer, one of which is recorded in John's Gospel, and other times, sweating as he does in Gethsemane. The whole range of human feelings, even post-traumatic human feelings, lived in him. These feelings are still with him. Just as the visible scars from the nails are still on his hands, feet, and side, so his invisible wounds are there too. This is what it means to be human.

There is a large group of traumatized people, perhaps the largest group, who work hard to minimize their trauma. "It really wasn't that bad compared to others." "No one actually did it to me." These statements distance them from what actually happened. They bring little relief, but traumatized people continue to say them. "It was just a trial, he only threatened me, he never hurt me." Jesus' trial shows us how threats are traumatic. In this trial we see all the shame, humiliation, disdain, and blame that is heaped upon him. It is the world's revenge, served cold, in the middle of the night.

The strangest part of this trial for me is Jesus' silence. In my anger, rage, and thirst for being understood, I would have shouted back against these accusations. And yet Jesus is silent. He is walking in the prophecies that say he will go like a lamb to the slaughter, silently. He does this willingly, self-consciously. He is enacting a larger story of redemption. His own retorts fade away in this prophetic light. He has committed his life to the God he prayed to his whole life, and no more words need to be spoken.

There is a holy silence. It is not the silence of shame or humiliation, the silence that comes when we think no one will believe us. It is not the silence of a victim, but of a martyr who is bearing witness with bravery and fortitude.

For me, Jesus' silence is my antidote story. I first read about antidote stories in Larry Dewey's *Trauma and Redemption*.[2] For many victims of trauma, a story of heroism or love within a traumatic event can help heal the pain of a traumatic memory. This is beyond mere positive thinking and may involve

meditation or therapies similar to Eye Movement Desensitiza-
tion and Reprocessing (EMDR) in which the patient visualizes
a truly safe space and tries to calm their central nervous system.
The silence of Jesus in his trial helps me with the traumatic
memory of the crucifixion, an event I have lived in my whole
life as a Christian.

As the church collectively meditates on the crucifixion
through art, music, sermons, and books, we may discover that
it contains our antidote story. The love, bravery, and ground-
edness of Jesus at his trial can inspire us in our chaos.

27

Mini-Sermons from the Cross

We come full circle to Skull Hill, back to the scene of the trauma. Here Jesus receives his five traumas, five wounds, to which his body still bears witness. It is here we meditate on the sights, smells, sounds, and the beating of our own hearts.

His seven words from the cross mirror the seven days of creation. Just as the seven days of creation happened with seven words, "And God said, Let there be . . . ," so these seven words are the unmaking of creation, as creation murders its God.

Preachers throughout Christian history have taken these seven words to their pulpits and exposited them before their congregations. I confess I always recall them in the King James Version, ingrained in my memory with all their power. This dramatic story can bear it all—the sins of the whole world. More than the sights, smells, and sounds, these seven words spoken aloud take us there as no film can do.

1. "FATHER, FORGIVE THEM; FOR THEY KNOW NOT WHAT THEY DO" (LUKE 23:34)

This one is hard to believe. The soldier who placed his knee on Jesus' neck while the nails were driven into his hands knew what he did. Those who orchestrated his trial knew what they did. Pilate, of all the characters in the story, said he knew what he did. All of them knew. All of us know.

Forgiveness fantasies are "cruel tortures." Like revenge fantasies, they remain out of reach for most human beings. The fantasy of forgiveness, like the fantasy of revenge, gives the victim the illusion of control and power, writes Herman.[1] However, it is hollow, empty, and may expose them to worse harm. Examples abound, and they all make us weep. Traumatized victims may dream, but those dreams remain dreams. Revenge and forgiveness exist in the fictional world, not in the real one. The moment I bring up the word "forgiveness," voices will be raised in protest. (*The first rule of forgiveness club is you do not talk about forgiveness club.*) Why would you demand, or even suggest, that someone forgive their abuser or rapist? Demanding forgiveness be given is like locking the victim in a room with the villain. Calls or demands for forgiveness are a form of unwitting abuse.

Forgiveness only works in situations that are unforgivable. Everything else is just forgetting. It cannot be demanded, and no one forgives by following someone else's formula. Christians are like everyone else; we don't forget things. Forgiveness cannot be demanded, mandated, even encouraged. We must step back from victims when we feel the impulse to tell them to forgive. If forgiveness comes, it must come from them. Accounts of pastors demanding wives go back to abusive husbands to be beaten or killed abound.

This statement from Jesus' cross, "Father, forgive them; for they know not what they do" is a speech-act in which the words are inseparable from the action. Jesus has power to forgive sin, and he uses that power in the most absurd place, his execution. In this one instance, forgiveness moves outside the realm of fantasy and into reality. While forgiveness is impossible for us, this one example lingers in the shadows of our consciousness, calling us to its possibility. That is all it can do—nothing more, nothing less. The post-traumatic Jesus forgives. That is all we need to know. His twisted body on the rough cross becomes the symbol of forgiveness. We hold it between our bodies and our perpetrators as if warding off a vampire. Our hands shake from the knowledge it may be possible for us, but we shrink back when we think of the practicalities involved.

Only the post-traumatic Jesus can forgive. Only the post-traumatic Jesus can be an example of how we might attempt such a thing. This Jesus cannot be reasoned with. His forgiveness flows from his very real wounds in body and soul. His blood is running out onto the ground when he speaks these words. All we can do is watch, listen, ponder, meditate.

2. "VERILY I SAY UNTO THEE, TODAY SHALT THOU BE WITH ME IN PARADISE" (LUKE 23:43)

The ease of this conversation always compels me. The two criminals who are crucified with Jesus hold a little trial of their own. I once heard an account of an execution in an Asian jungle. The observer watched the condemned man being led to his death by two guards who held him by his arms. The condemned man was wearing flip-flops, and when he came to a puddle, he skipped his step to avoid putting his foot in the mud. The observer reflected that even in this moment before all moments are to end, the human being cares about a muddy foot. We are people, human beings, to the bitter end, whatever that end may be.

These two criminals feel their life drain out and still jaw jack, banter, shoot the breeze like they were back on the block. Such is the banality of cruelty on Skull Hill. The last words of the condemned are like this—so ordinary, and at the same time so profound.

"Jesus, remember me when you come into your kingdom" is a statement of faith alongside our most venerable creeds. There is nothing left to lose when the criminal says this. This is the creed of the traumatized, from one dying human to another dying human.

If PTSD is a memory issue, characterized by intrusive thoughts and flashbacks, then it is our remembering that is wounded. The wounded memory is a wound of our soul, the place where our meaning lives. That he would ask Jesus to remember him means he is asking Jesus to remember his pain as well as his own life. This is what Jesus does. Even as he remembers us, he remembers the pain. They are forever inseparable.

No matter how much healing we experience, the trauma of trauma is never diminished or reduced. It will always stand in its monstrous horror, but in that horror we remember and we are remembered.

3. "WOMAN, BEHOLD THY SON! . . . [SON,] BEHOLD THY MOTHER!" (JOHN 19:26–27)

While Jesus' trauma is center stage in the Gospel narratives, Mary's trauma enfolds his as only a mother's can. Living with your heart outside your body is how mothers describe it. There is no separation between bodies. You hurt when they hurt.

Mary's trauma was prophesied, as so much trauma is in the world of the Bible and elsewhere. Shortly after Jesus is born, an old man in the Temple says to her, "A sword will pierce your soul" (Luke 2:35). With each stab of her soul, did Mary wonder if that was the big one? Standing by the cross, she knows this is it. This is the piercing. Her soul is being skewered.

The practicalities of this statement cannot be ignored. Jesus, as the eldest son, was responsible for his mother, and now that responsibility passes to the beloved disciple. Trauma rewrites relationships and social norms. The disciple is now the eldest son. Jesus is powerless in his trauma, pinned down by the nails. He is helpless to perform the basic functions of life, another hallmark of trauma.

In this transfer of responsibility, Mary becomes the mother of those who hang from nails. She comes to us in our trauma and loss and knows what it feels like to be pinned down, helpless, immovable. She is silent with us as she is at the cross and her heart beats with love, even while it drips blood from the sword embedded in it.

4. "ELOI, ELOI, LAMA SABACHTHANI?" (MARK 15:34)

Jesus quotes the first line of a sad song from his cross. "My God, my God, why have you forsaken me?" is the first line of Psalm 22. He quotes it in the vernacular Aramaic translation from the Hebrew. It was this line that came to him at that particular moment, as only song lyrics can come to us. The DJ in our mind pulls out the one record we need to hear in that moment and plays it. What plays for you in these moments?

Yes, there are prophetic echoes here in this psalm that Jesus is enacting as Messiah, but I cannot escape that he hears music in his trauma. Maybe it's because I've heard the music.

Songs come to us when we need them. Perhaps this is God with us in our trauma in some small way. When Paul and Silas are brutally beaten and imprisoned in stocks, they sing (Acts 16:25). Their songs echo in the hole they have been put in. A song on the lips is the last act of defiance we can muster in our pain and death.

We will never hear this song the same way again.

The next Psalm after 22 is 23: "The Lord is my shepherd; I shall not want. He maketh me to lie down in green pastures; he leadeth me beside the still waters. He restoreth my soul" (23:1–3 KJV). Can any greater contrast be drawn? The song of being abandoned by God followed by the song about how God cares so much for us? The emotional range of songs is infinite—the deepest valley to the highest mountain in one concert. We sing along as the music echoes in our heads.

Sometimes we look for rational solutions for our post-traumatic distresses, when the gift was right there all along, humming in the back of our minds.

5. "I THIRST" (JOHN 19:28)

In pain and torment, we are reduced to the most basic of needs. Gone is the existential quest for meaning, for harmony, for significance. All we can think about is the location of our pain as it moves around our body on its own dreadful schedule.

The cruelty of Jesus' crucifixion is on display as he croaks for water. His voice joins the delirious voices whimpering for water on the Devil's Highway as they attempt to enter the United States undetected. The heat of the sun on an exposed body will cook the brain, as all bodily systems begin to shut down to preserve sanity.

The voice of Jesus crying "I thirst" joins the chorus of hoarse voices who cry for their basic needs as they die under the indifferent sun. His voice is not alone. It is our voice too, a voice that God hears.

6. "IT IS FINISHED" (JOHN 19:30)

Is it ever really over? The answer for Jesus and for us is yes and no. Yes, his six-hour ordeal ended, but that is when his post-traumatic journey began. The ongoing aftermath of 9/11 killed the concept of "closure," which should have been killed earlier as it was always an illusion.

When I first started taking medication for PTSD, I told myself again and again, "This is until I'm better." I couldn't accept the reality that I would have this, or something like this, until I died. I didn't want to be dependent on pills. I don't know when I accepted the long-term nature of my illness, my new life, but once I did, it was easier to take the pills. I even took the Rev. Nigel Mumford's counsel to say grace over my pills before taking them. Medicine is a food and food is a medicine, all to be injected as from the hand of God to us. Give us this day our daily dose.

While a high school commencement marks the end of an education, the word *commencement* means "beginning." The ending is the beginning, and it is at this moment on the cross that we meet the post-traumatic Jesus. He is silent. He has said all he can say. He is all wound and blood. And we can be sure this wounded Jesus is the one we can follow.

7. "FATHER, INTO THY HANDS I COMMEND MY SPIRIT" (LUKE 23:46)

Victims of trauma often say how powerless they felt. The freeze response kicks in, and there is disassociation from one's own body. The separation of soul and body is what we call death, and the body prepares for it. Even the comfort of being dead is a sad mercy, the last defense against an unstoppable onslaught.

This final gasp of Jesus, reported as a loud cry in several accounts, is a handing over of himself. It is a delivery to the inevitability of death. It is also a statement of faith, as it assumes the Father will catch him.

Was not this the temptation on the pinnacle of the Temple? Cast yourself down, says the tempter, your Father will catch you. Jesus refused the bait then, quoting the Scripture text that says we should not tempt God. But now, on this cross, he is falling from a great height. In his final breath he knows he will be caught, grasped, held.

In his final breath, he is no longer just a victim; he is an actor. From the confines of the four nails he dances, twirls, fascinates. He is an agent, a participant, and Lord of all. We stare at this from a distance and see that even at our most helpless moments we can still do what he does—commend our spirit to God's hands.

Every night, Christians (especially in monastic traditions) have prayed the Compline office, the final night prayers before sleep. "Into thy hands I commend my spirit" is from Psalm 31. We quote this with Jesus from his cross, knowing him in the fellowship of his crucifixion and death as we come closest to death in sleep, itself an ancient euphemism for death. This is what we are afraid of—death—and it is something we now have a say about.

28

Post-Traumatic Witness

I have spent most of my adult life as a soldier, and so when I read the crucifixion story, I find myself identifying with the soldiers in the story even more than I find myself identifying with the disciples. The life of a soldier in any era is a life lived close to suffering. When I think of World War I coming to an end, I cannot comprehend the scale of the suffering. Millions died, ground into the mud of No Man's Land in a war that seemed pointless to everyone involved. This war became known as the Great War, the war to end all wars, and yet it did not end all wars.

The nations suffered the losses of their finest young people, and the suffering of that war became enshrined in the twentieth century as the turning point in so many lives. That military service is a particular kind of suffering is a point driven home in the literature that emerged from the Great War. The haunting poetry and pain-filled novels showed us that up close.

But there was suffering in homecoming too.

"England looked strange to us returned soldiers," wrote World War I veteran Robert Graves. "We could not understand the war-madness that ran wild everywhere, looking for a pseudo-military outlet. The civilians talked a foreign language. I found serious conversation impossible."[1]

When my parents signed my enlistment papers as witnesses because I was only seventeen, I found out that military service is about suffering. Since I had to first graduate from high school, I attended numerous Saturday meetings where Marine Corps drill instructors spent a couple of hours getting us recruits ready for boot camp. We did exercises while they critiqued our form. I still get nervous when the yoga teacher comes over now, thinking they're going to yell at me. I would be sore for days after these workouts. It was the first of many sufferings.

There was the suffering of getting up at 4:30 a.m. the day after my high school graduation and my recruiter taking me to the Military Entrance Processing Station (MEPS) in Philadelphia, swearing in there, and then flying to Parris Island, South Carolina, where I got off the bus from the airport at zero dark thirty. The drill instructors screamed at us as we hustled off the bus to stand on the yellow footprints. I didn't have a summer; I had boot camp.

There was the suffering of missing a semester of college because a military assignment didn't end in time.

There was the suffering of that frigid night in the mountains when I was sitting in a hole in the ground freezing my ass off—and the snow turned into freezing rain.

There was the suffering of not going to my grandfather's funeral because I was doing important training.

There was the suffering of saying good-bye to my two sons and wife to go to Iraq and then coming back and watching my youngest recoil in horror when I went to hug him.

There was the suffering of finding out that one of my soldiers had killed himself, and that soldiers in my unit had gotten blown up—then feeling the twisted relief that only two had died, a small number compared to worse explosions. Or the suffering of being in a really hot place and wearing armor and missing home, missing a world without war, and not being able to remember what it was like.

And there was the suffering of coming home and not feeling a thing, of not switching on the switches I had switched off over there—the switches that make family life possible, that make joy possible. There was the suffering of finding out my wife had a boyfriend, our neighbor, a fellow married Army officer who outranked me, and that somehow this was my fault.

There was the suffering of being a chaplain on the psych ward at Walter Reed National Military Medical Center and the suffering of the amputee ward, both visible witnesses to the suffering of our whole military family and our nation. There was the suffering of feeling like I don't belong here in this world, that I should be dead, that nothing good will ever happen in my life and I might as well end it all.

But none of these sufferings were anything like the sufferings of Christ.

Well, maybe one was.

There was the night when I went out on my porch and told God how I felt; when I asked God why he had turned his almighty back on me; why he didn't care about my marriage, or my family, or my soul, or anything; when I said, "My God, my God, why have you forsaken me?" Maybe then some of my sufferings crept a little closer to the sufferings of Christ, who said those same words from the cross.

As much as I think of myself as someone who has suffered, I also caused suffering—immense suffering—and I cannot lie about this. You grow up thinking you want to be Luke Sky-walker, but you wake up one day and realize you're one of the storm troopers. I was part of an army that occupied a foreign land, and we were cruel, even as we tried to build a better Iraq.

Cruelty is survival in an occupation like that, and the longer I reflect on those days the more I realize I am not so much like Jesus of Nazareth, suffering on the cross, but more like one of the soldiers who nailed him to the cross. I am the soldier who pierced his side, using a thrust I learned at Parris Island in that summer after my high school graduation. I know who I am and what I did.

I am also like those soldiers who draped a scarlet robe over his shoulders and put a crown of thorns on his head until he bled, and I'm like those soldiers who mocked him and spit on him and who beat him again and again, as only those who have had others be cruel to them can do. And I'm like those soldiers who gambled for his clothes, and guarded him while the world looked on, and taunted him while he said, "Father, forgive them; for they know not what they do."

I'm like those soldiers. And like those soldiers who did all those things, I believed. The first people to believe in Jesus after his crucifixion were the soldiers who crucified him. Matthew's Gospel says, "When the centurion and those with him, who were keeping watch over Jesus, saw the earthquake and what took place, they were terrified and said, 'Truly this man was God's Son!'" (27:54). Surely, he was the son of God.

The Marine Corps and the Army didn't pay me to think. They taught me to act on what I saw. And I've seen it. I've seen Jesus on the cross, I know he is the son of God. I know that now, and I want to follow him. I want to follow him in his suffering for love. I want to follow him in the way he lived. I want to follow him in how he forgave his enemies. I want to follow him to the cross. I want to bring some reconciliation to this war-torn world. I want to announce the good news that no matter what you've done or no matter what you've left undone, Jesus is praying, "Father, forgive them; for they know not what they do" for you.

I want to announce to a suffering world that there is consolation in God when you suffer, that you are not alone on this planet, that you are not alone in your sufferings, that you are greatly loved—greatly loved. And you have a place in this family—this fellowship of forgiven sufferers—this community of God's love. This place saved my life.

We remember the post-traumatic C. S. Lewis asking after coming home from the horrors of World War I, "What call have I to dream of anything? . . . Our throats can bark for slaughter: cannot sing."[2]

Only a crucified, suffering, post-traumatic Jesus can heal us so we can sing again. So sing, my friends. You who have been wounded by war and homecoming, violence and cruelty. In Lewis's epic children's fairy tale *The Chronicles of Narnia*, he has Aslan create the world with a long and beautiful song. We can sing again.

29

Cleaning Up the Mess

Every Sunday morning, I insist that two people carry the bread and the wine forward so we can set the table for Communion. It's not always practical, since both tiny containers of wine and bread could easily be carried by one person. Some have insisted on carrying both. It's no big deal; they're small, they say. But we insist that one person carries the bread and one person carries the wine because of what happened just moments after the crucifixion of Jesus.

The DSM-5 says PTSD is caused by exposure to traumatic events. One of the ways people are exposed includes "experiencing repeated or extreme exposure to aversive details of the traumatic event(s) (e.g., first responders collecting human remains; police officers repeatedly exposed to details of child abuse)."[1] Medics in my Army unit in Iraq were responsible for collecting human remains after an attack. They picked up hands, feet, and other body parts at the scene. Then they cleaned out the armored vehicles with powerful detergents, attempting to mask the smell. Two men do something similar for Jesus after his death: Joseph of Arimathea and Nicodemus.

This is why two people carry the bread and wine in church, because two people carried the broken body of Jesus on that first Good Friday. It is simple, simplistic even, to commemorate this event this way. But simple is good in the aftermath of trauma. We do not need complex solutions. First, we need love, kindness, and the gentle, careful way two men hold the human remains of their teacher.

Mister Rogers famously said about what to do after a horrific event, "Look for the helpers." And we do that when we contemplate what these two do for Jesus. We reenact their trauma so that a bridge is built across the ages to connect them to us. We see the post-traumatic Jesus through their eyes; we feel him with their hands.

In some way, when we carry the bread or wine in church, we are loving the post-traumatic Jesus. At its most basic, primal level, this is worship—ascribing value to something the world has beaten, tortured, and cast aside. If Jesus were not carried by these men, his body would likely have gone to the dump in some unmarked hole in the ground. These men save what is left of him, just as God saves what is left of us in the aftermath of trauma.

The walk from the back of the church to the altar offers us a time to reflect on the ones who carried our post-traumatic selves—in body or in spirit—who offered us a kind word, a place to stay, or the silence of understanding. As time goes by and we get further and further from our traumatic event, these small gifts of love grow in our minds.

The people who carried us can grow larger, their small acts of love growing to fill the emptiness of our sorrow. Against the blood-drenched backdrop of our horrific days, their love stands out as a gift from a silent God. And this too is God, this very human love. Incarnations of love exist around us, and they are called people. We are also incarnations of love, the enfleshment of love. When my chance to love comes, I hope I take it.

30

Post-Traumatic Resurrection

One second after he breathed his last on the cross, the post-traumatic Jesus was born—his cradle a tomb, his swaddling clothes a shroud. Of course, every second of his earthly life was lived in the literary shadow of the cross, since his biographers saw his life this way, but now, in these final chapters, we see what he is like post-trauma.

Like a butterfly undergoing metamorphosis, he comes out of the tomb in a new and glorious way. If his outward appearance is changed significantly, could not his inner life be rearranged too? What triggers someone who has been crucified?

One personality change I see in him through my post-traumatic lens is that he seems to have more personal authority. He does not argue or debate the way he sometimes does in Gospel accounts. When people encounter him, they are often speechless, stunned, questioning. He speaks to them with authority, with even a bigger twinkle in his eye. At least, that is how I read it.

After the road to Emmaus encounter, Jesus asks the disciples, "Why are you troubled, and why do doubts arise in your hearts? See my hands and my feet, that it is I myself" (Luke 24:38–39a ESV). He can see their traumatized response. It is written on every surface of their faces; it is in every nervous gesture. Their bodies are keeping the score, and it is easy to see.

If Jesus can see this in them, he can see it in us. He sees our tics, our twitches, our glances at the door. He sees us sweat, get headaches, get in the car and go home. Nothing is hidden from the post-traumatic Jesus—nothing. He meets his disciples in the first days of their trauma, and he meets us there too.

That he shares meals with so many people after the trauma of the cross should be expected. Jesus fed people; he ate and drank with people, as all accounts make clear. His behavior is consistent, even though his post-traumatic meals are campfire cookouts, impromptu taste tests (they hand him a piece of broiled fish to eat), and a broken loaf in an inn. A full meal may be too much. Again, Jesus meets them where they are, at their level of comfort and safety.

His calling card is his wounds, his trauma: "See my hands and my feet, that it is I myself." The wounds are healed, we suspect, although it is not entirely clear from the texts. Jesus does, after all, invite Thomas to put his hand into his side-wound.

Getting close to Jesus' five wounds has been a quest of the church since it began. Whether it is medieval relics in a Roman Catholic grotto or a Baptist passion play, the faithful seek his wounds. The church exists in the side-wound of Jesus, safe and protected. It is from whence we are birthed, like Adam birthing Eve out of his riven side. We are born in this wound, out of this wound, and we return to this wound in times of distress. The post-traumatic Jesus has given us a building not made with hands—his own wounded body. It is in this wound that we are safe, wounded though we are. Like Jesus, our wounds are our calling cards for inclusion, not marks of estrangement and alienation.

Healing does not mean scars and wounds go away. Healing means we have a new life. That new life is limited by our scars and wounds, but it is profoundly more meaningful than it was before the moment that changed us forever. That Jesus' wounds are still visible should tell us something profound about the nature of healing and our new life following the post-traumatic Jesus.

Questions for Discussion

Individuals with PTSD, C-PTSD, or other extreme trauma experiences should study this book in a group with other traumatized people, not with readers who do not share experiences of trauma.

1. Was there a time in your life when you experienced excruciating physical or emotional pain? Do you consider yourself to be in recovery from traumatic events?

2. Where did you first hear or read the story of the crucifixion of Jesus? Do you remember what you felt when you first heard it?

3. Where are you on Skull Hill? Which person in the crucifixion story do you most identify with today?

4. What Bible story covered in this book resonated with you most strongly? Do you share trauma symptoms with a character in that story?

5. The Roman Empire was a source of trauma for many people in Jesus' world. Is there a looming, oppressive force functioning as a "Roman Empire" in your post-traumatic experience? What do those forces have in common?

6. Loss of trust is such a common and significant symptom of trauma. Did any stories in this book give you hope for finding faith and trust again?

7. In what ways are you tempted like Jesus in the wilderness? How do you cope with such temptations?

8. Has your experience of church or religion in general been affected by trauma? In what ways?

9. Which of the Beatitudes speak to you most strongly? When you think of them not aspirationally but descriptively, do you find you are already among the "blessed"?

10. The author says, "Shame doesn't give freedom, only more entanglement. Freedom is found in leaving and following" (p. 34). What do you need to leave, and what do you need to follow?

11. Have you experienced what the DSM-5 calls "persistent and exaggerated negative beliefs or expectations about oneself, others, or the world"? How has this symptom affected the way you pray?

12. Reflecting on the Last Supper and Psalm 23:5, "You prepare a table before me in the presence of my enemies," how does trauma affect your eating habits, especially in communal settings?

13. How has trauma affected your relationships with others? Do you identify more with the demon-afflicted man living alone in the graveyard (Mark 5) or the woman caught in adultery (John 8)?

14. How do you receive Jesus' admonition to "put away your sword"? Is your "sword" a metaphorical or a physical weapon?

15. Does a need for forgiveness play a role in your trauma recovery? Whom do you need to forgive? From whom do you long for forgiveness?

16. Which of Jesus' "Seven Last Words" do you most need to hear? Why?

17. How does reflecting on Jesus' resurrection transform the way you think about his crucifixion? What healing metamorphosis might you imagine for yourself?

Notes

Introduction

1. Elizabeth Boase and Christopher G. Frechette, eds., *Bible through the Lens of Trauma* (Atlanta: SBL Press, 2016).

Chapter 1: Skull Hill

1. William Shakespeare, *Hamlet, Prince of Denmark* (London: Bradbury and Evans, 1859), 93.
2. Mary Beard, *SPQR: A History of Ancient Rome* (New York: Liveright, 2015), 16.

Chapter 2: Announcing the Prince of Peace in a World of War

1. Adrian Goldsworthy, *Pax Romana: War, Peace, and Conquest in the Roman World* (New Haven: Yale University Press, 2016), 1.
2. Tacitus, *The Germany and Agricola of Tacitus,* trans. Edward Brooks Jr. (Philadelphia: David McKay Publishers, 1897), 122.
3. Judith Herman, *Trauma and Recovery: The Aftermath of Violence—from Domestic Abuse to Political Terror* (New York: Basic Books, 1992), 161.

Chapter 3: Post-Traumatic Christmas

1. Sigmund Freud, *Beyond the Pleasure Principle,* trans. James Strachey (London: Hogarth Press, 1955), 35.
2. Bessel Van Der Kolk, *The Body Keeps the Score* (New York: Penguin Publishing, 2015).

Chapter 4: Dreams and Nightmares

1. Flavius Josephus, *The Complete Works of Flavius Josephus,* trans. William Whiston (London: T. Nelson and Sons, 1860), 591.

2. Josephus, *Complete Works of Flavius Josephus*, 405.

3. Josephus, *Complete Works of Flavius Josephus*, 412.

4. Josephus, *Complete Works of Flavius Josephus*, 419.

5. The Jewish Encyclopedia "Mariamne," (New York: Funk and Wagnalls, 1906), 332.

6. Judith Herman, *Trauma and Recovery: The Aftermath of Violence—from Domestic Abuse to Political Terror* (New York: Basic Books, 1992), 39.

Chapter 5: The First Temptation

1. Luis Alberto Urrea, *The Devil's Highway* (New York: Little, Brown, 2004), 82.

2. Rollo May, *The Meaning of Anxiety* (New York: Norton, 1977), 80.

3. George Cowe Holt, *November of the Soul: The Enigma of Suicide* (New York: Scribner, 2006), 340.

Chapter 6: Come and Die

1. Jonathan Shay, *Achilles in Vietnam: Combat Trauma and the Undoing of Character* (New York: Scribner, 2010), xx.

Chapter 7: Healing Dis-ease

1. Walter Scheidel, ed., *The Science of Roman History: Biology, Climate, and the Future of the Past* (Princeton, NJ: Princeton University Press, 2018), 25.

2. Kyle Harper, *The Fate of Rome: Climate, Disease, and the End of an Empire* (Princeton, NJ: Princeton University Press, 2017), 100.

3. Harper, *Fate of Rome*, 101.

Chapter 8: The Beatitudes: A Trauma Manifesto

1. Miroslav Volf, *Free of Charge: Giving and Forgiving in a Culture Stripped of Grace* (Grand Rapids, MI: Zondervan, 2005), 158.

2. Christopher B. Zeichman, ed., *Essential Essays for the Study of the Military in First-Century Palestine: Soldiers and the New Testament Context* (Eugene, OR: Pickwick Publications, 2019), 9.

Chapter 9: The Traumatized Samaritan

1. Flavius Josephus, *The Complete Works of Flavius Josephus*, trans. William Whiston (London: T. Nelson and Sons, 1860), 611.
2. Ali Parchmani, *Hegemonic Peace and Empire: The Pax Romana, Britannica, and Americana* (New York: Routledge, 2009), 21.
3. Judith Herman, *Trauma and Recovery: The Aftermath of Violence—from Domestic Abuse to Political Terror* (New York: Basic Books, 1992), 42.
4. Herman, *Trauma and Recovery*, 42.

Chapter 10: Post-Traumatic Invitation to "Take Up Your Cross"

1. C. S. Lewis, "French Nocturne (Monchy-Le-Preux)," *Best Poems Encyclopedia*, https://www.best-poems.net/c-s-lewis/french-nocturne-monchy-le-preux.html.
2. Judith Herman, *Trauma and Recovery: The Aftermath of Violence—from Domestic Abuse to Political Terror* (New York: Basic Books, 1992), 92.
3. Elie Wiesel, *Night*, memorial ed., trans. Marion Wiesel (New York: Hill and Wang, 2017), 34.

Chapter 12: Are Women Human?

1. Flavius Josephus, *The Complete Works of Flavius Josephus*, trans. William Whiston (London: T. Nelson and Sons, 1860), 698.
2. Judith Herman, *Trauma and Recovery: The Aftermath of Violence—from Domestic Abuse to Political Terror* (New York: Basic Books, 1992), 13–14.

Chapter 13: Parable of the Traumatized Son

1. Bob Dylan, "Tryin' to Get to Heaven," *Time Out of Mind*, Columbia Records, 1997.

Chapter 14: Healing the Traumatized Daughter

1. Judith Herman, *Trauma and Recovery: The Aftermath of Violence—from Domestic Abuse to Political Terror* (New York: Basic Books, 1992), 97.

2. Walter Wink, *Engaging the Powers: Discernment and Resistance in an Age of Domination* (Minneapolis: Augsburg Fortress, 1992), 12.

Chapter 15: Post-Traumatic Exorcism

1. Aristotle, *The History of Animals*, trans. D'Arcy Wentworth Thompson. Book III: 19.
2. Michael Yandell, "'Do Not Torment Me:' The Morally Injured Geresene Demoniac," in *Exploring Moral Injury in Sacred Texts*, ed. Joseph McDonald (London: Jessica Kingsley Publishers, 2017), 135.
3. Judith Herman, *Trauma and Recovery: The Aftermath of Violence—from Domestic Abuse to Political Terror* (New York: Basic Books, 1992), 109.

Chapter 17: The Friend at Midnight

1. American Psychiatric Association, *Diagnostic and Statistical Manual of Mental Disorders,* 5th ed. (Arlington, VA: American Psychiatric Association, 2013), 171–72.
2. Paul Tillich, *The Courage to Be* (New Haven, CT: Yale University Press, 1952), 190.

Chapter 19: Post-Traumatic Adultery

1. Dennis Ortman, *Transcending Post-Infidelity Stress Disorder: The Six Stages of Healing* (New York: Random House, 2009).

Chapter 20: The Donkey King

1. Søren Kierkegaard, *Either/Or*, trans. Alastair Hannay (New York: Penguin, 1992), 43.
2. Tim O'Brien, *The Things They Carried* (New York: Houghton Mifflin, 1990), 64.

Chapter 21: Hypervigilance

1. Judith Herman, *Trauma and Recovery: The Aftermath of Violence—from Domestic Abuse to Political Terror* (New York: Basic Books, 1992), 86.

Chapter 22: Post-Traumatic Judas

1. Michael Card, "Traitor's Look," *The Life*, Sony Music, 1987.

Chapter 23: The Lasting Supper

1. Judith Herman, *Trauma and Recovery: The Aftermath of Violence—from Domestic Abuse to Political Terror* (New York: Basic Books, 1992), 107.

Chapter 25: Post-Traumatic Cold

1. Judith Herman, *Trauma and Recovery: The Aftermath of Violence—from Domestic Abuse to Political Terror* (New York: Basic Books, 1992), 3.

Chapter 26: Post-Traumatic Trial

1. Judith Herman, *Trauma and Recovery: The Aftermath of Violence—from Domestic Abuse to Political Terror* (New York: Basic Books, 1992), 72.

2. Larry Dewey, *War and Redemption: Treatment and Recovery in Combat-Related Posttraumatic Stress Disorder* (Burlington, VT, Ashgate Press, 2004), 173–86.

Chapter 27: Mini-Sermons from the Cross

1. Judith Herman, *Trauma and Recovery: The Aftermath of Violence—from Domestic Abuse to Political Terror* (New York: Basic Books, 1992), 198.

Chapter 28: Post-Traumatic Witness

1. Quoted in Chris Baldick, *The Oxford English Literary History: 1910-1940*, vol. 10, *The Modern Movement* (Oxford: Oxford University Press, 2002), 188.

2. C. S. Lewis, *Best Poems Encyclopedia*, https://www.best-poems .net/c-s-lewis/french-nocturne-monchy-le-preux.html.

Chapter 29: Cleaning Up the Mess

1. American Psychiatric Association, *Diagnostic and Statistical Manual of Mental Disorders*, 5th ed. (Arlington, VA: American Psychiatric Association, 2013): 171–72.

CPSIA information can be obtained
at www.ICGtesting.com
Printed in the USA
LVHW021125210123
737639LV00004B/9

9 780664 267322